The Carver's Handbook:

Carving The Wild Life of the Forest and Jungle

by David E. Pergrin

Schiffer Publishing Ltd

To my devoted wife, Peggy, whose keen sense of shape, size and color has aided immeasurably in my carving efforts.

Library of Congress Catalog Number: 84—52153

Printed in the United States of America.
ISBN: 0-88740-029-9
Published by Schiffer Publishing Ltd. 1469 Morstein Road, West Chester, Pennsylvania 19380

This book may be purchased from the publisher.
Please include $1.50 postage.
Try your bookstore first.

Table of Contents

Preface 4

The Tiger 5

The American Goldfinch 27

The Wood Mouse 39

The Great Horned Owl, Relief Carving 49

Preface

The purpose of *The Carvers' Handbook* is to provide teachers and students in the woodcarving field with a fundamental system of instruction. I hope this will enable all to enjoy this rapidly developing American realistic form of art.

We will explore all of the modern tools used to carve, texture and paint wood carvings of wild life.

A series of relief carvings and figures in the round are presented to satisfy the requirements for the Boy Scout woodcarving merit badge. Realistic color photographs of each carving and the patterns to develop the carvings are shown so that the carver can visualize the finished project while the work is in progress.

This is the second book in the Carvers' Handbook Series. Instructions are presented for carving a tiger, a goldfinch, and a mouse in the round and an owl in relief.

David E. Pergrin

The Tiger

Materials And Tools Needed

Carving knife
Band saw or Coping saw.
Dremel Tool with high speed cutting heads. Nos. 115, 118, 125, 131, 193, 194 & 196
Mandrel for sanding drums. No. 407
Sander bands. Nos. 408 & 432.

Burning pen with rheostat control
Basswood block 2" x 10" x 5½"
Glass eyes, 3mm
Carbon paper
Pencil
Paint brushes Nos. 1, 2, & 3
Sandpaper

Acrylic paint
- Brilliant orange
- White
- Raw Sienna
- Yellow medium

Epoxy putty
Cardboard

The major feline of the Asian continent. The tigers *(Panthera tigris)* are the largest of the cats, but they are slimmer and narrower in the body than lions. The coat provides a natural camouflage against the patterns of light and shade in natural surroundings. The coat usually has the same basic coloring, the ground color being a shade of reddish fawn, broken at intervals by dark vertical stripes. The belly is white, and there are patches of white on the face.

Fossils show that the tiger originated in Siberia and then spread south to occupy most of Asia and parts of Malaysia. A full grown tiger will eat 40-60 pounds of meat at one feed in the wild. A male can weigh 420 pounds and measure 9 feet 5 inches.

Carving the tiger using the wood from the American Linden tree will cause you to see the beauty of this majestic animal.

Before you start, go to the library and obtain some books that show colored pictures of the tiger.

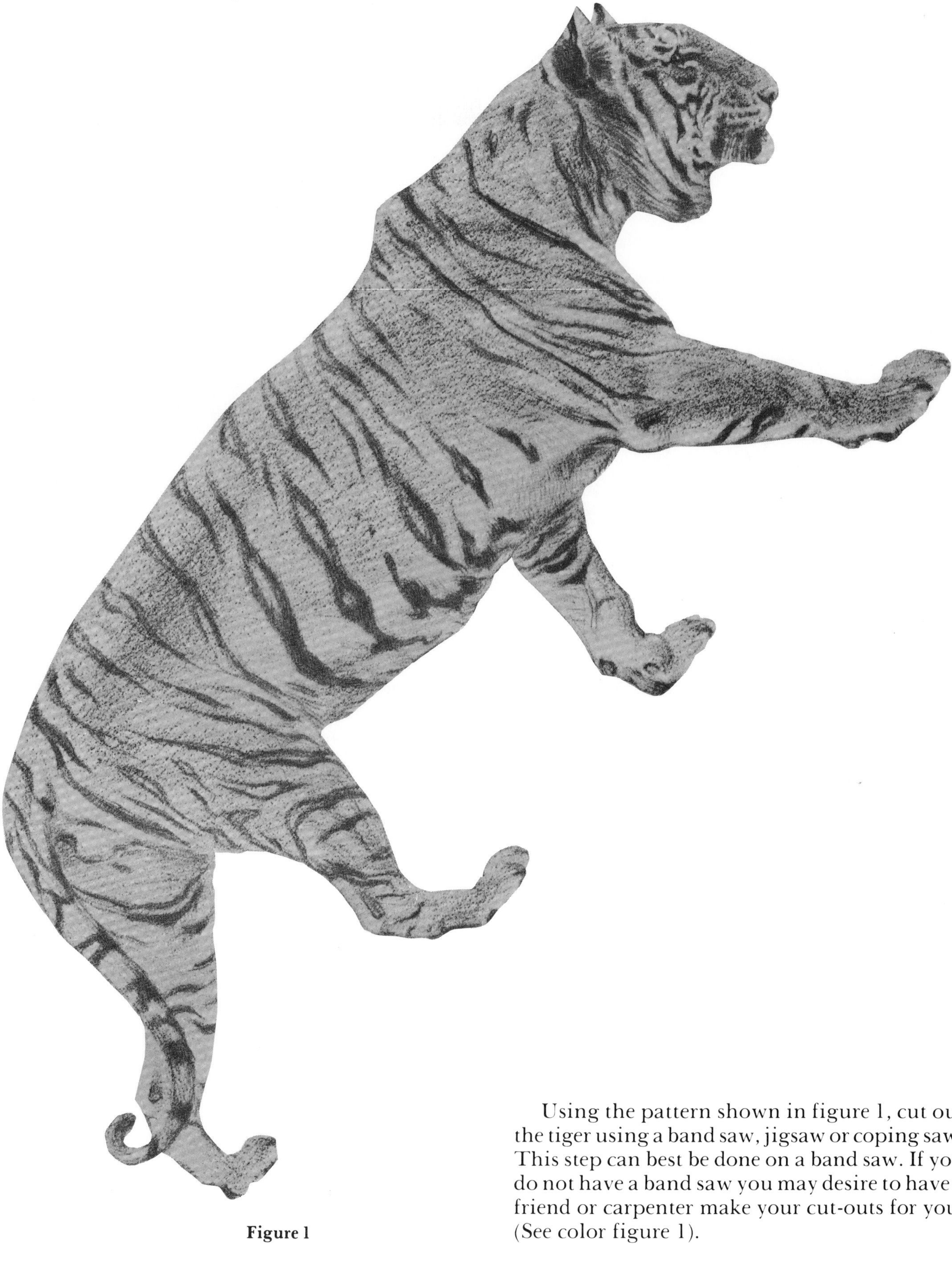

Figure 1

Using the pattern shown in figure 1, cut out the tiger using a band saw, jigsaw or coping saw. This step can best be done on a band saw. If you do not have a band saw you may desire to have a friend or carpenter make your cut-outs for you. (See color figure 1).

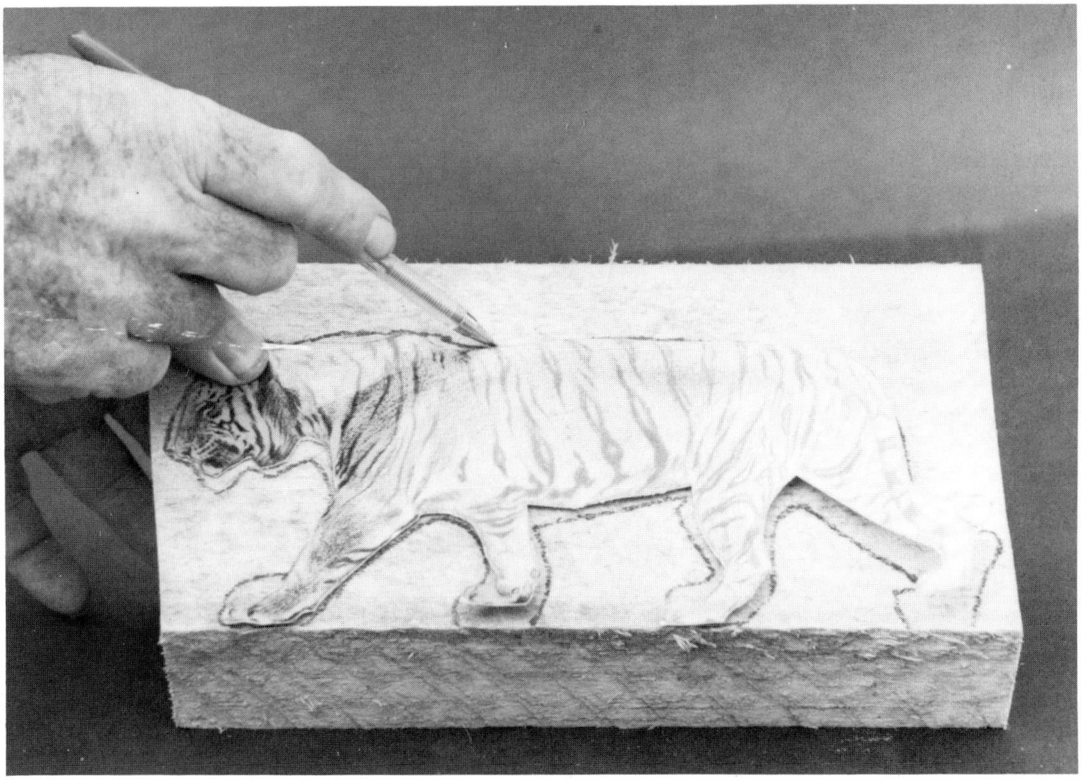

Figure 2

Trace the pattern on a basswood block 2" x 10" x 5 1/2".

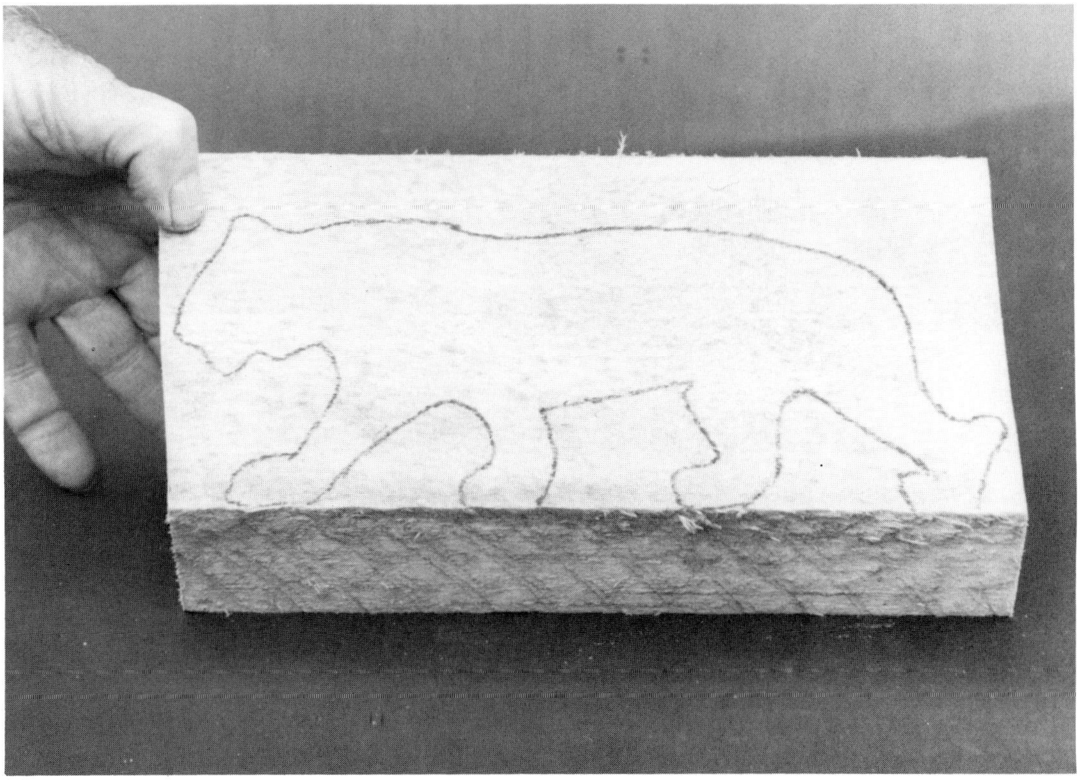

Figure 3

Tracing with heavy pencil line displayed clearly.

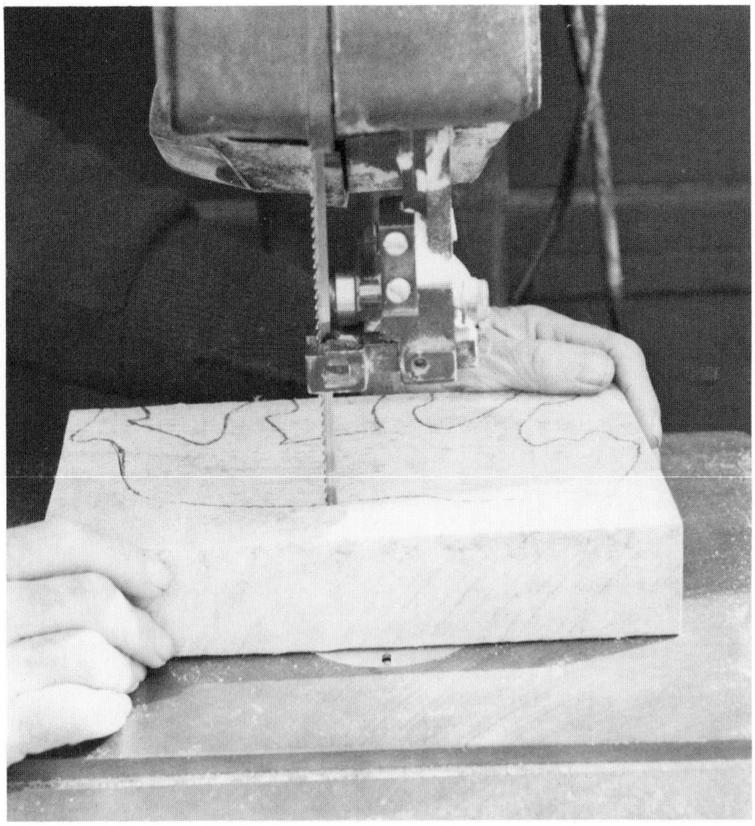

Figure 4

Cutting out the tiger using a 12 inch band saw.

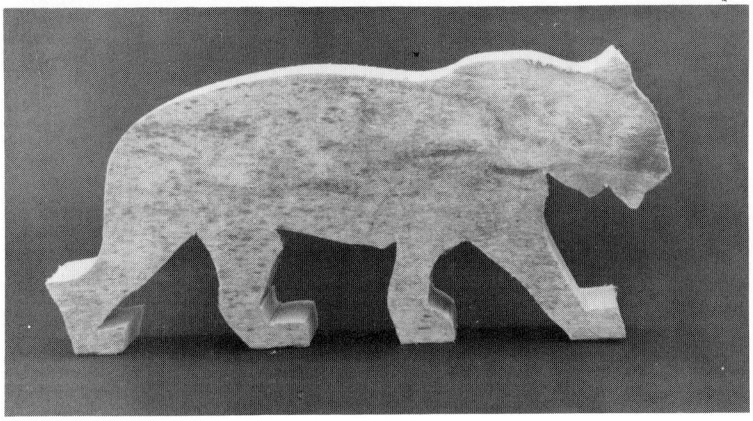

Figure 5

The tiger cutout complete ready to carve!

I have selected the Dremel Moto-Tool to make this carving and the following cutting heads which may be obtained at most hobby shops:

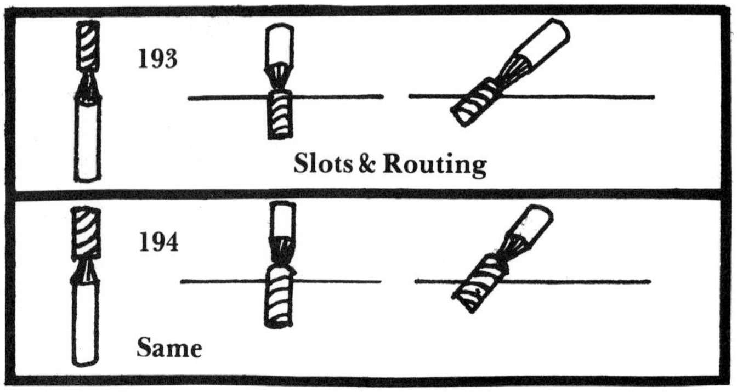

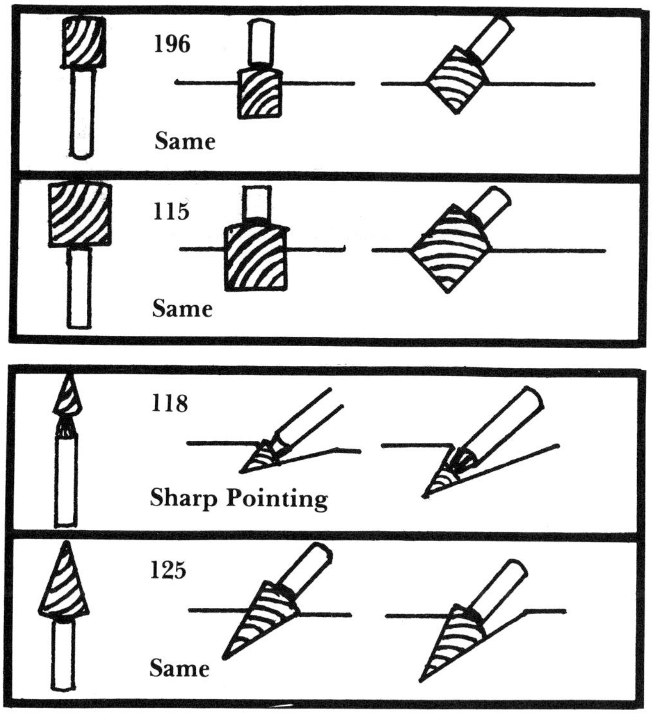

SANDING ACCESSORIES
can be used for big or small jobs...

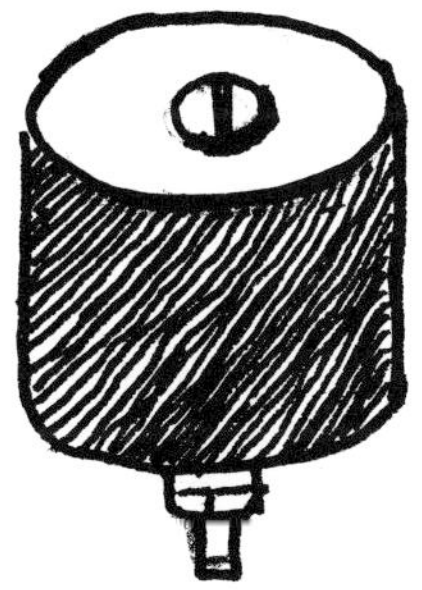

DRUM SANDER—No. 407
Ideal for rough shaping wood and smoothing fiber glass. Sander bands are replaceable in 1/2" sizes. Comes with one band. 1/8" shank.

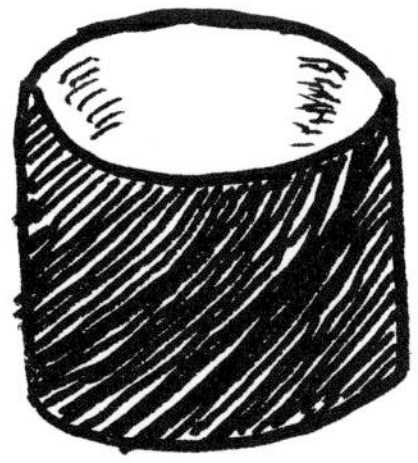

Drum Sander Bands
1/2" diameter coarse grit—No. 408
1/2" diameter fine grit—No. 432

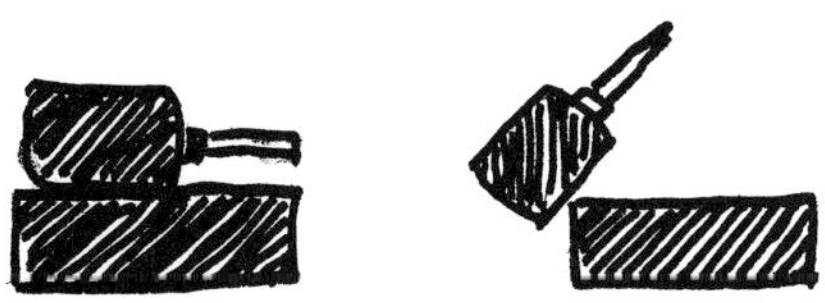

I have selected the moto-tool for three reasons. Safety, time saving, and accuracy.

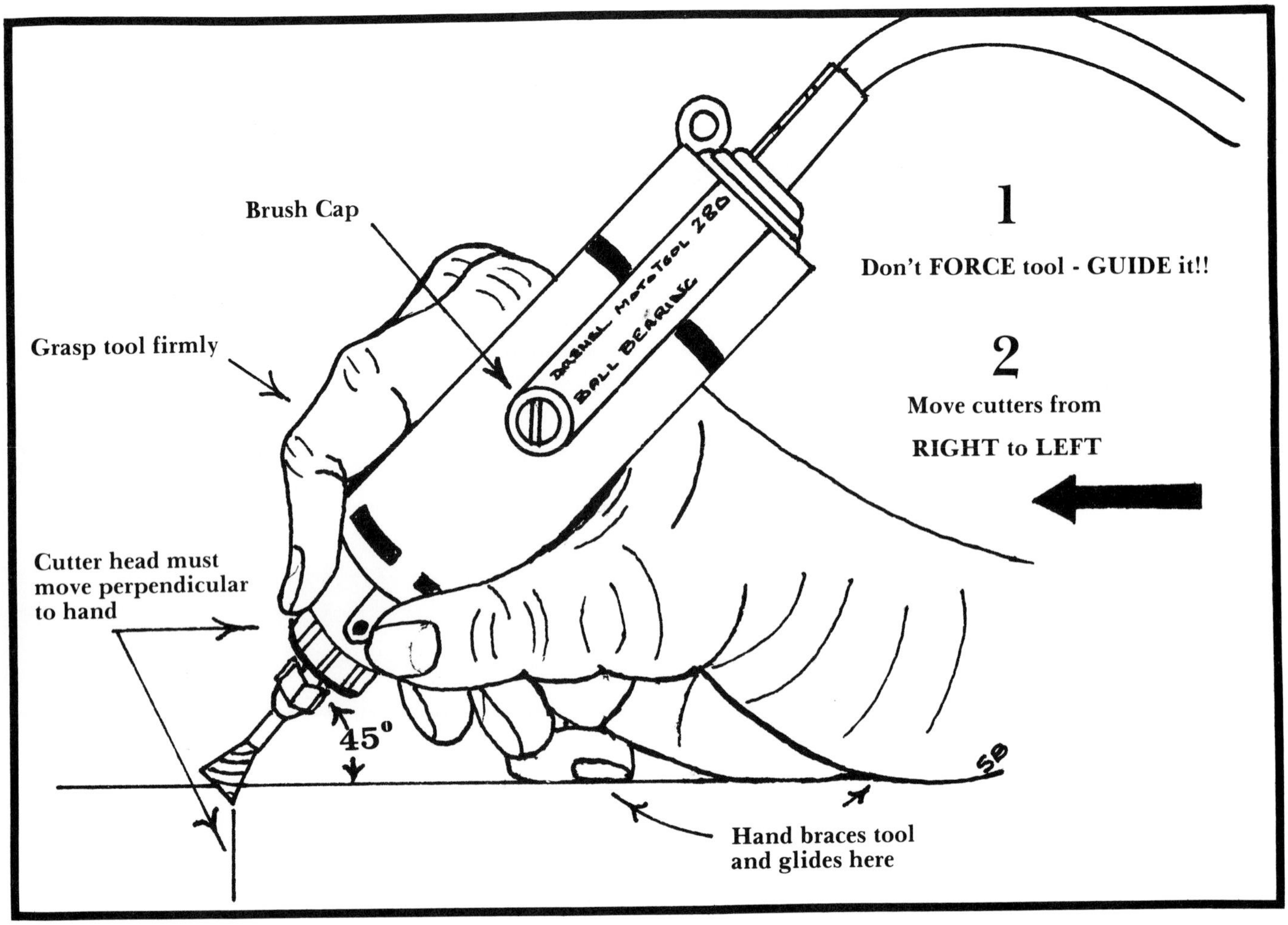

Figure 6

Proper method of using the moto-tool. I cannot overstress items 1 and 2 on the sketch.

My experience in teaching hundreds of beginners has caused the recommendation of this type tool. The tool can be either rotary grinder or flexible shaft.

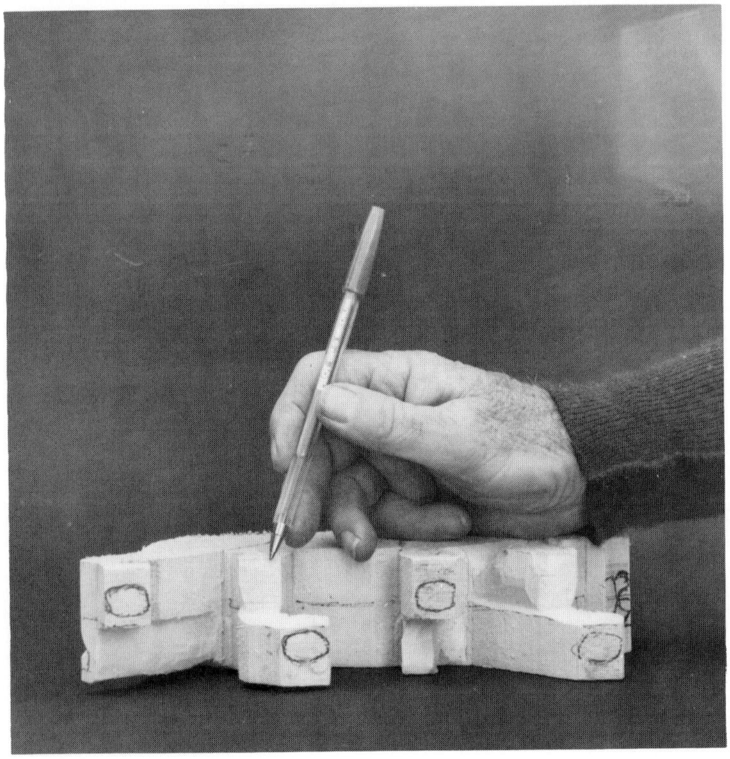

Figure 7

The first step is to draw in the center on the cutout as shown in figure 7. This also shows the four paws sketched on the bottom.

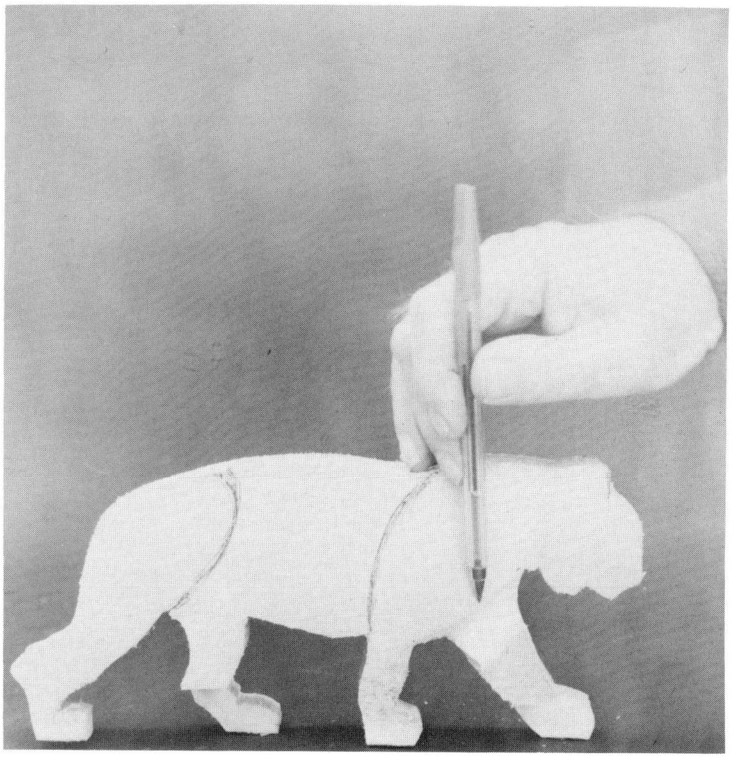

Figure 8

Shows sketching in the thigh muscles on the right hand side. Note that both front and rear legs are positioned towards the rear.

Figure 9

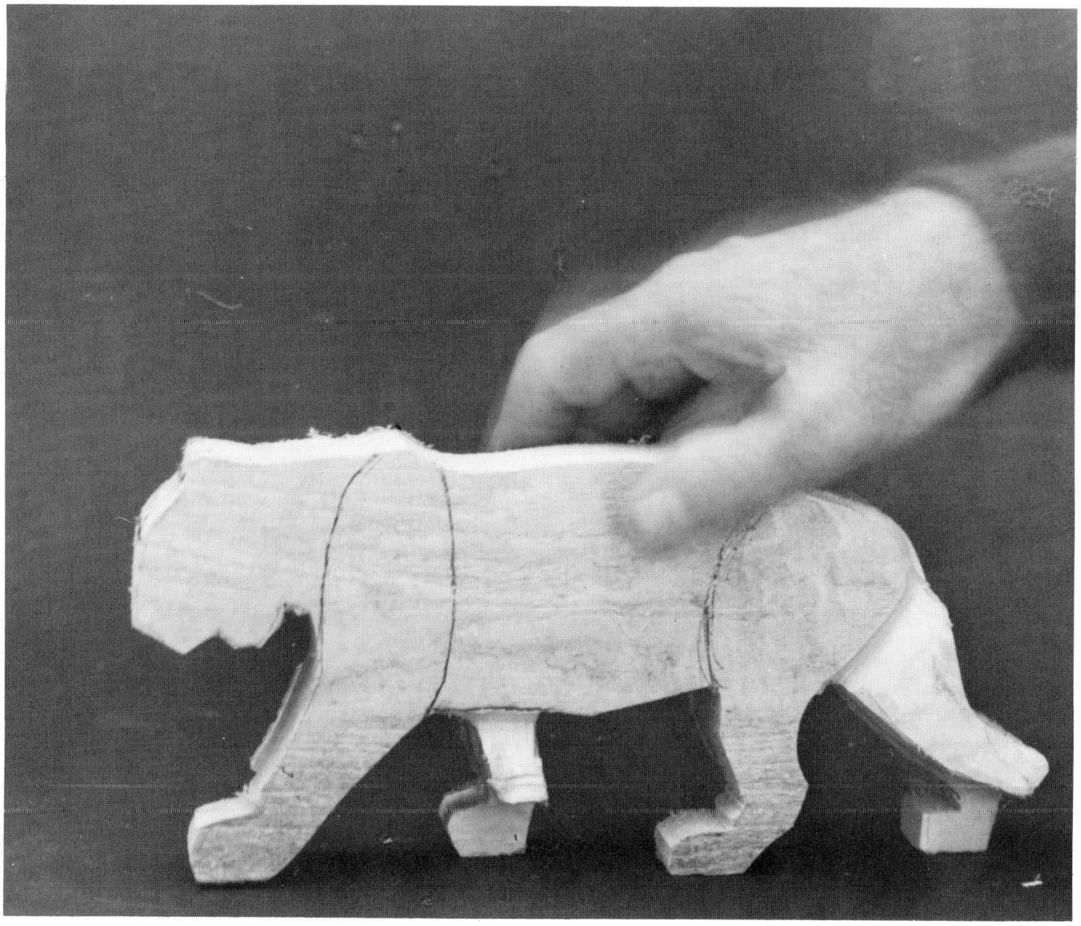

Markings of the thigh muscles on the left hand side.

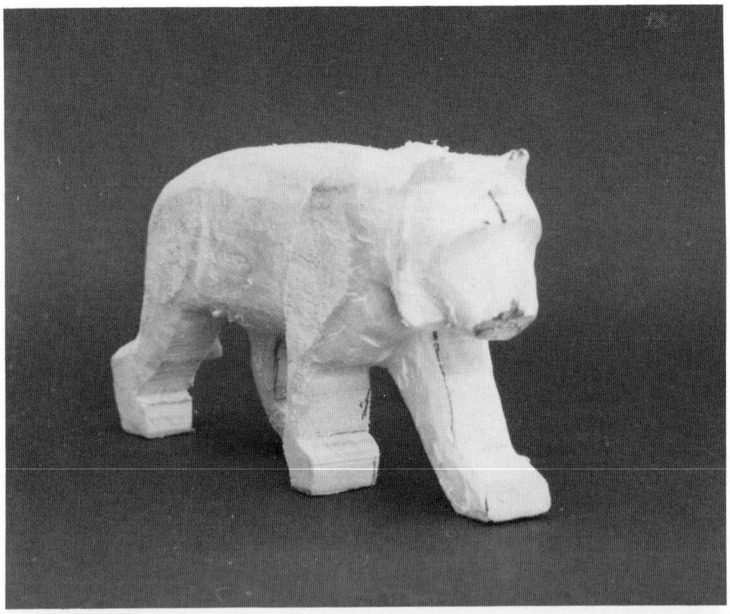

Using the moto-tool with carving bit Number 115 carve off the excess wood on the legs and shape the hips and thighs. The result of this effort is shown in figures 10 and 11. These two figures also show the shaping of the head and tail.

Figure 10

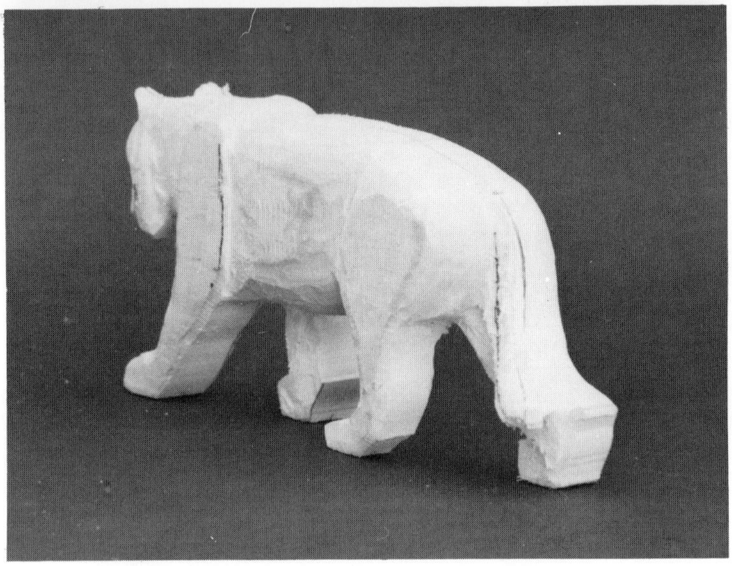

Figure 11

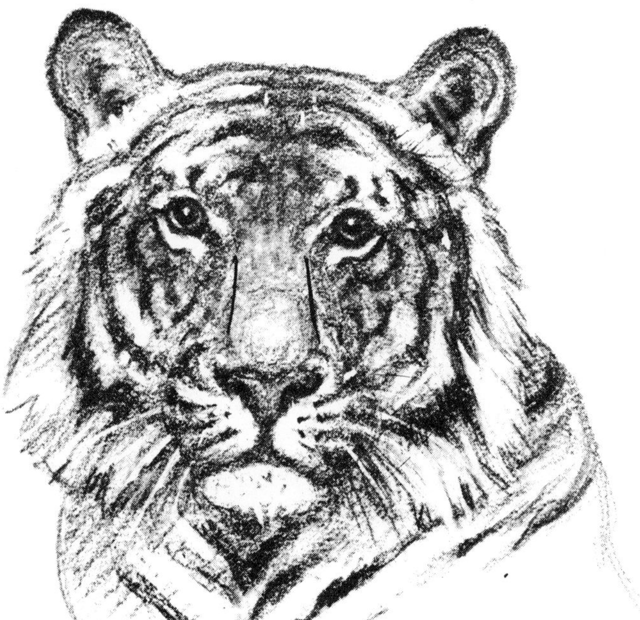

Figure 12

Front view of tiger's face.

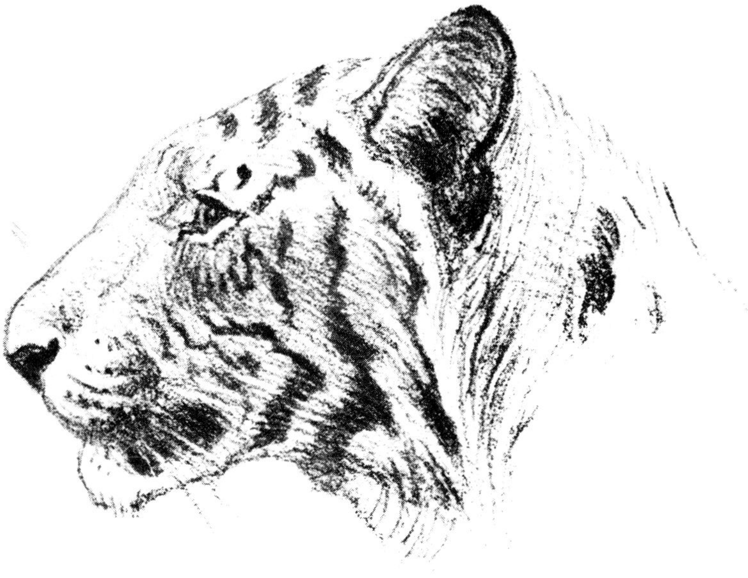

Figure 13

Profile view of tiger's face.

The sketches of the tiger's face are to aid you in drawing in the prominent features and to enable you to carve in the eyes, ears, nose and mouth in the proper position. A protractor can be very helpful!

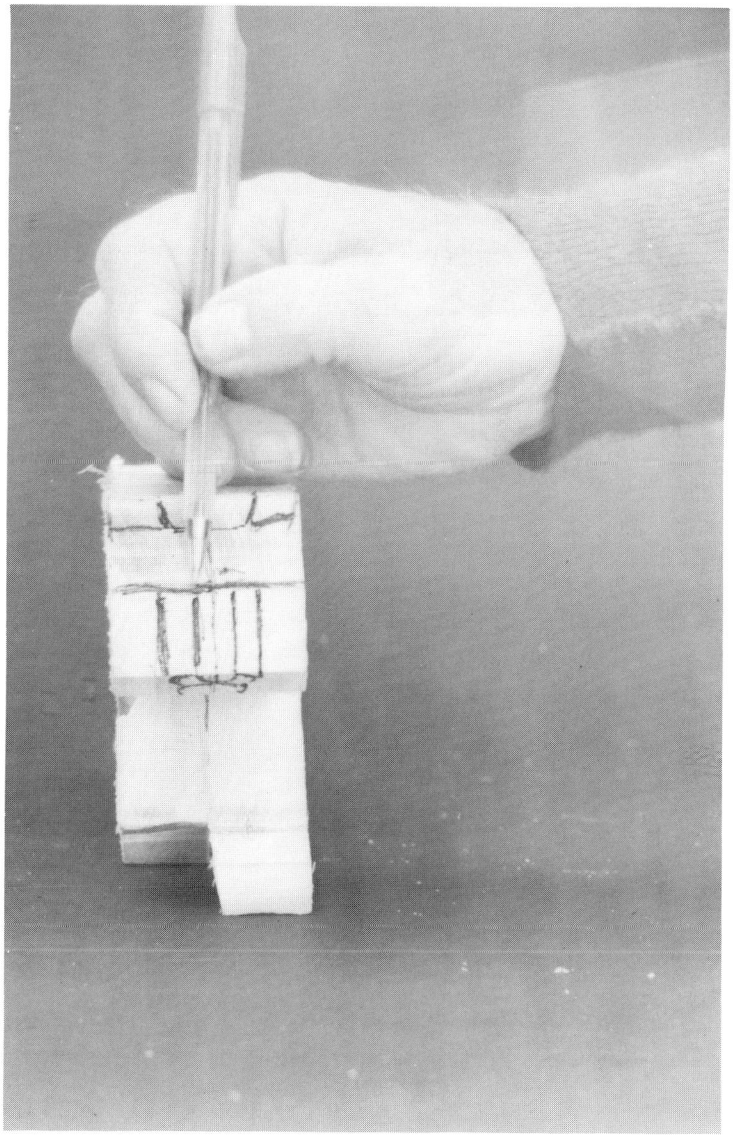

Figure 14

Showing lines drawn to develop the carving of the nose, cheek, and ears.

At this time study figures 15, 16, 17, and 18 and complete the detail as shown on these four positions of the tiger. Note the tail, the position of the ears, and the shaggy hair around the cheeks. Note the trim rounded under belly and the long snout above the cheek structure.

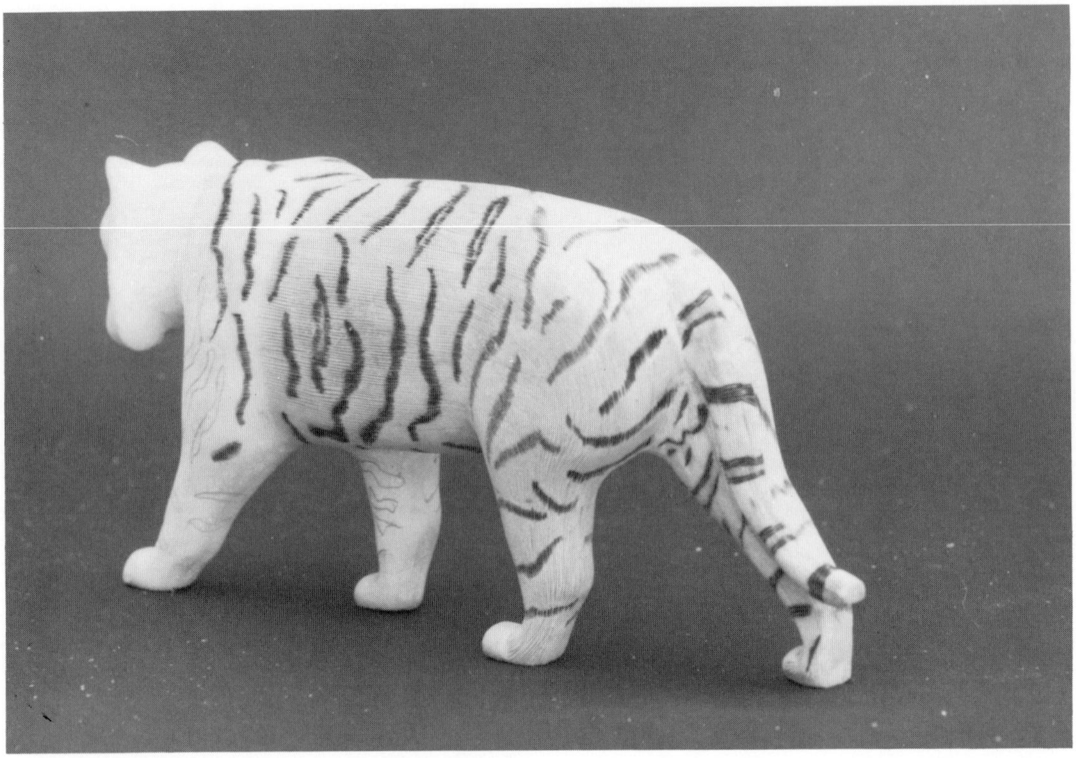

Figure 15

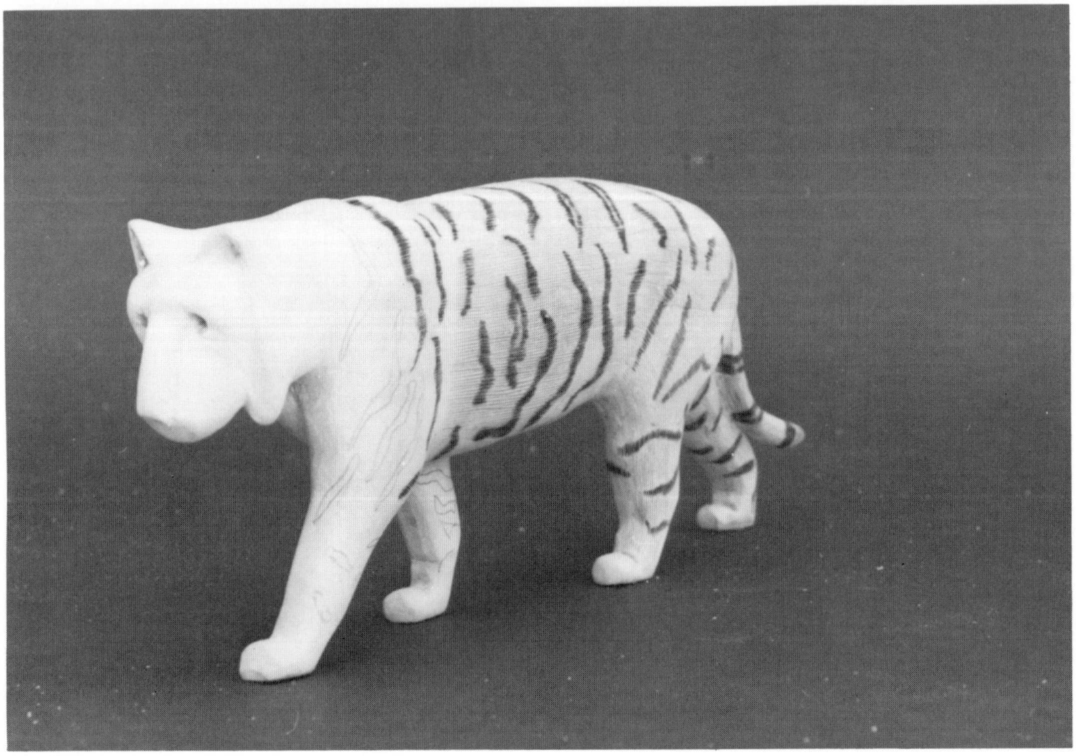

Figure 16

Figure 17

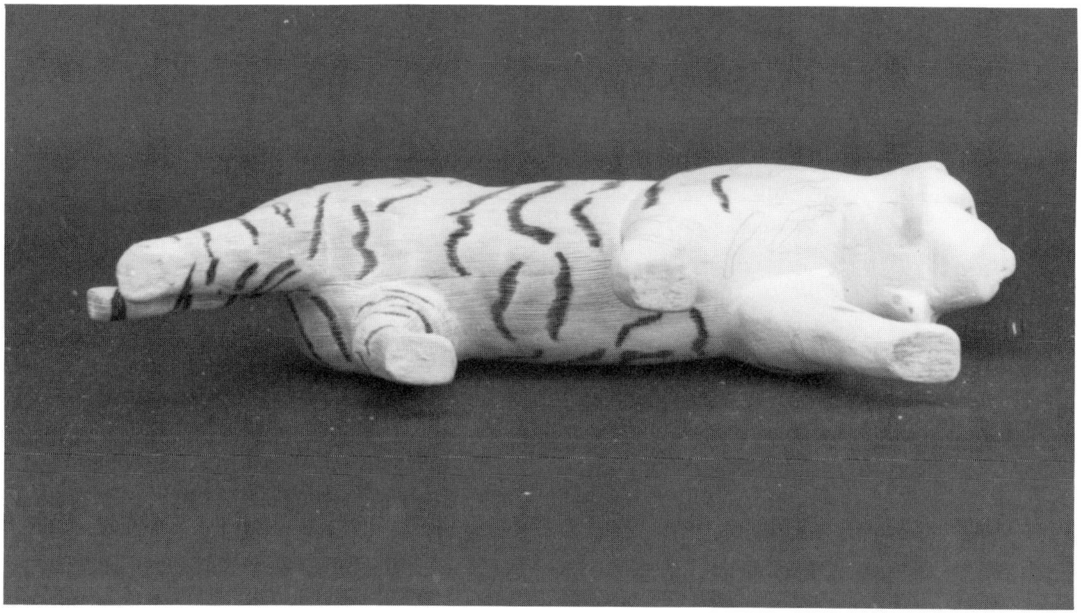

Figure 18

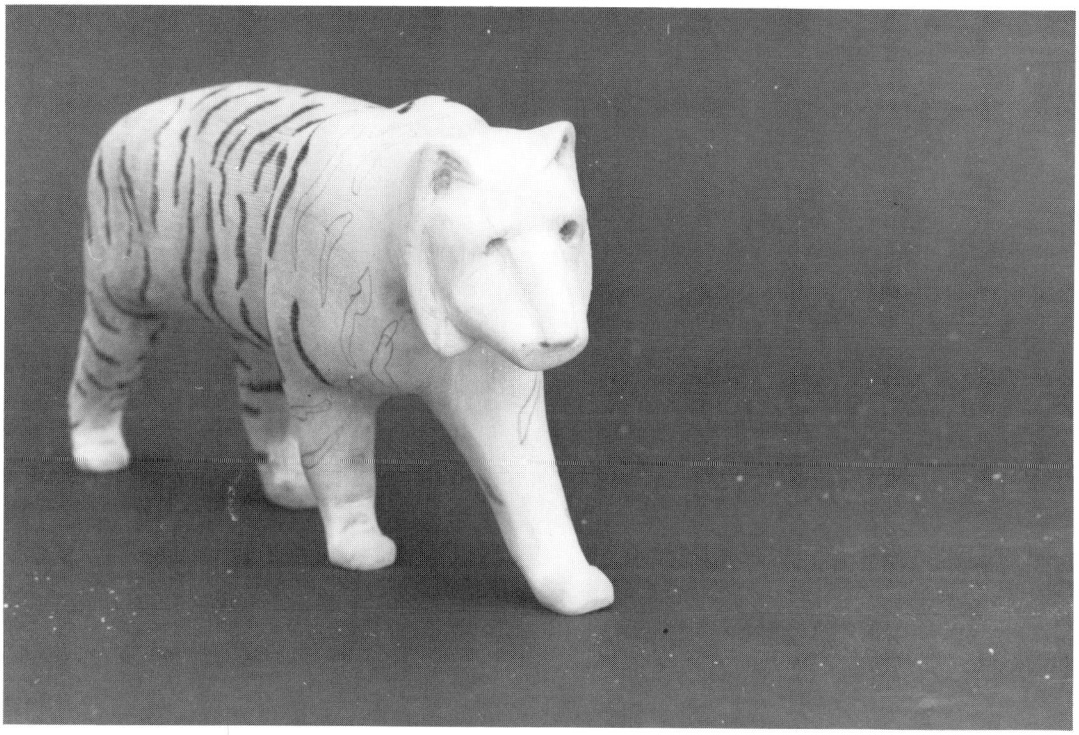

The very important step following the detail carving is to give the entire surface a smooth sanding job to remove uneven surfaces and fuzziness. Use No. 432 Drum sander band on rubber cushioned drum sander.

Do not force the moto-tool in the sanding operation. Only use light smooth right to left strokes. Bathe the carving in rubbing alcohol and let it dry for 15 minutes. Now hand sand with fine sand paper.

The next step is to insert the eyes. Using 3 mm clear glass eyes, paint the back side of the eyes yellow and clip off the wire leaving about 1/4 inch of wire on the glass eye. Dry the acrylic paint on the eye.

Using cutting head No. 194, drill in the eye sockets to a depth of more than 1/4 inch. Round out the eye sockets so that the glass eyes fit in flush. Fill the eye sockets with the epoxy putty mix leaving the mix level with the top of the hole.

Now insert the glass eyes level with the top of the eye socket and smooth out the excess putty. Using a knife, shape a slight lid at the top of the eye. This operation is shown in Figures 19, 20, and 21.

Figures 19, 20, and 21 demonstrate the method used to install the eyes.

Study the vertical dark lines on the pattern of the tiger. Sketch the dark lines on your carving with a pencil, and using a heavy setting on the burning pen texture the dark lines as shown in figure 15.

Set a low setting on the burning pen and texture the tiger completely with the pen producing a very light colored burn.

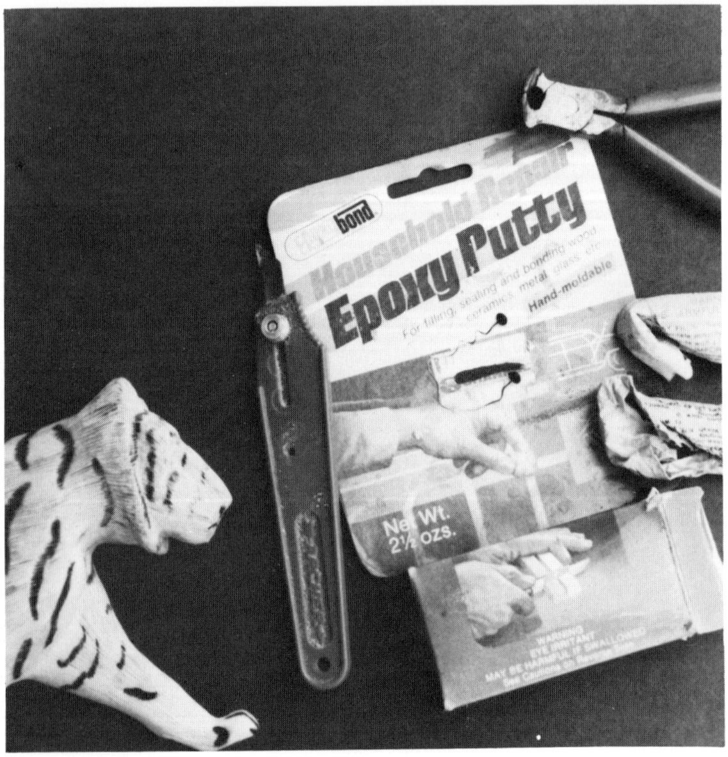

Figure 19

Material and tools used to install eyes. The clear glass (2 mm) eyes are painted yellow and are shown in the center of the picture.

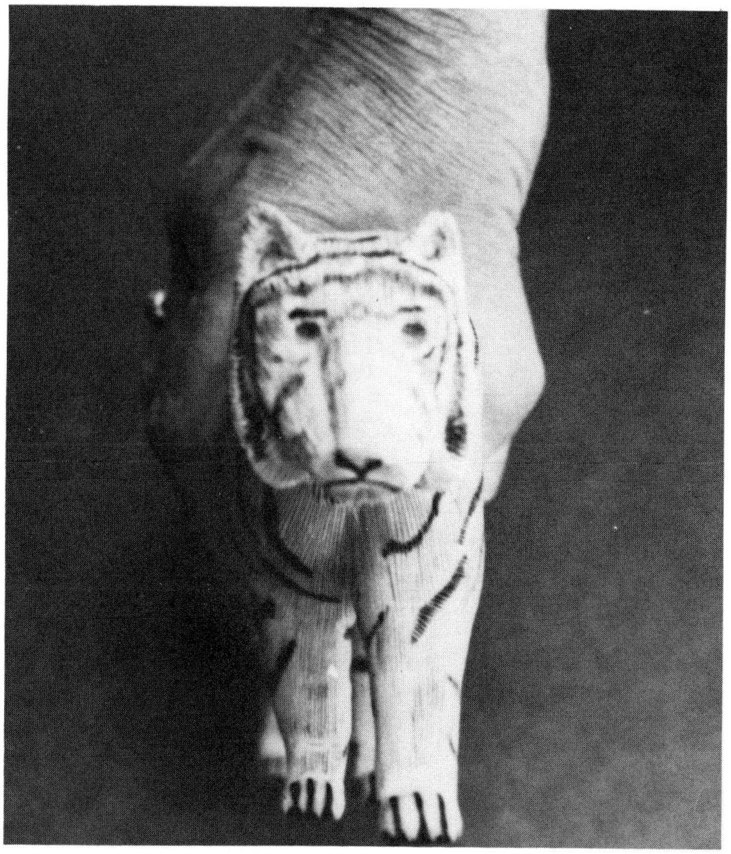

Figure 20
Eye sockets drilled.

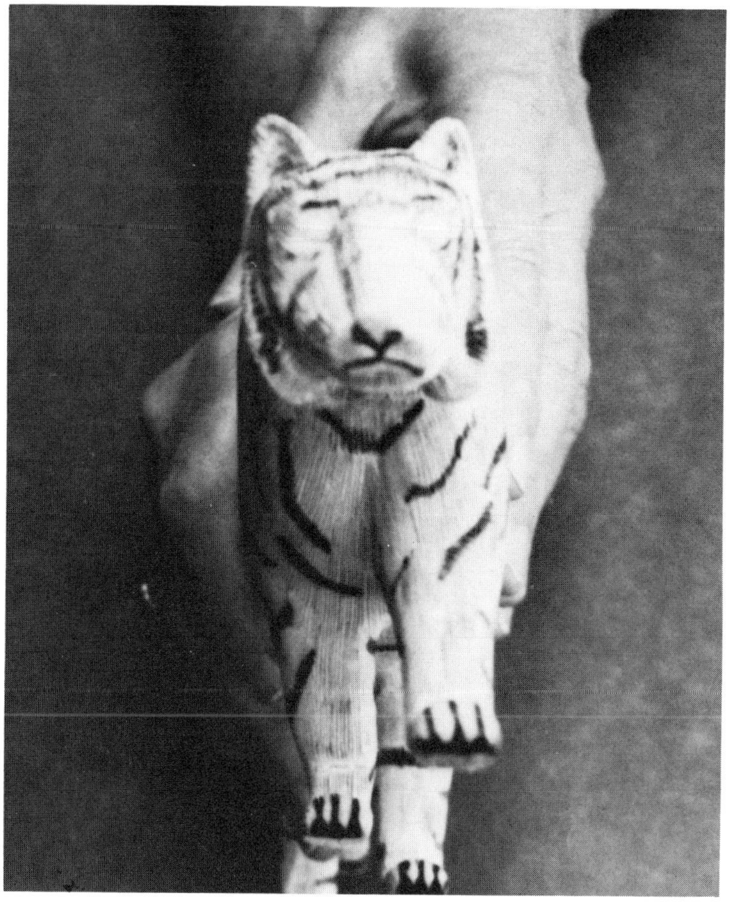

Figure 21
Epoxy putty in eye sockets.

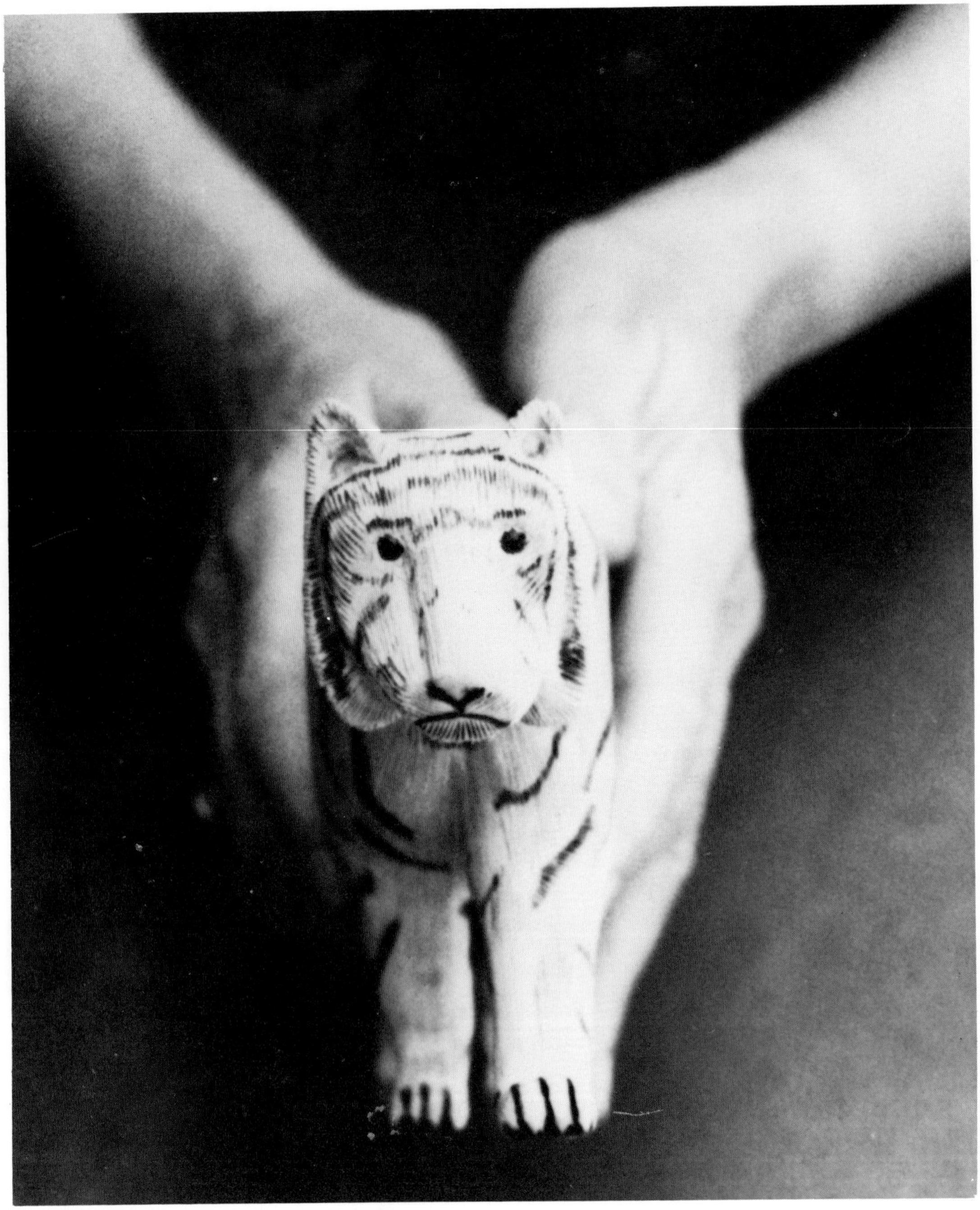

Figure 22

Eyes installed.

The final step is to paint the tiger using acrylic paints. Mix 2 inches of Brilliant orange with 1/2 inches of Raw Sienna just as it comes from the tube. Add a touch of water and paint the entire tiger between the verticle dark lines. Do not paint over the dark lines or on the underbelly as shown in Figure 23. Dry the entire carving and paint the 2nd coat of the tawny orange mix.

Now paint the underbelly and part way down on the inside of the legs. The mix is 10 parts titanium white and just a touch of Raw Sienna. Dry with a hair dryer and dry brush the sharp line between the underbelly and the body of the tiger!

Figure 23

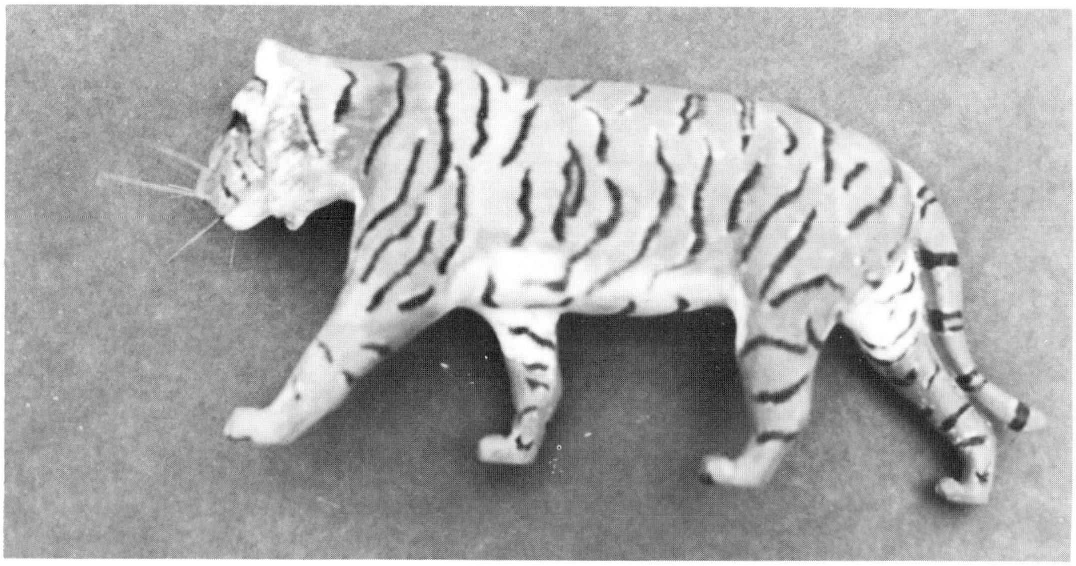

Note the area on the underbelly and inside of the legs which are painted white.

Your tiger will become more realistic when you cut eight 1 1/4" hairs from a light colored brush. Make four pin holes on each side of the snout. Dip the end of each hair in quick drying glue and insert the hairs in the eight pin holes. The tiger is now finished — complete with whiskers!

Figure 24

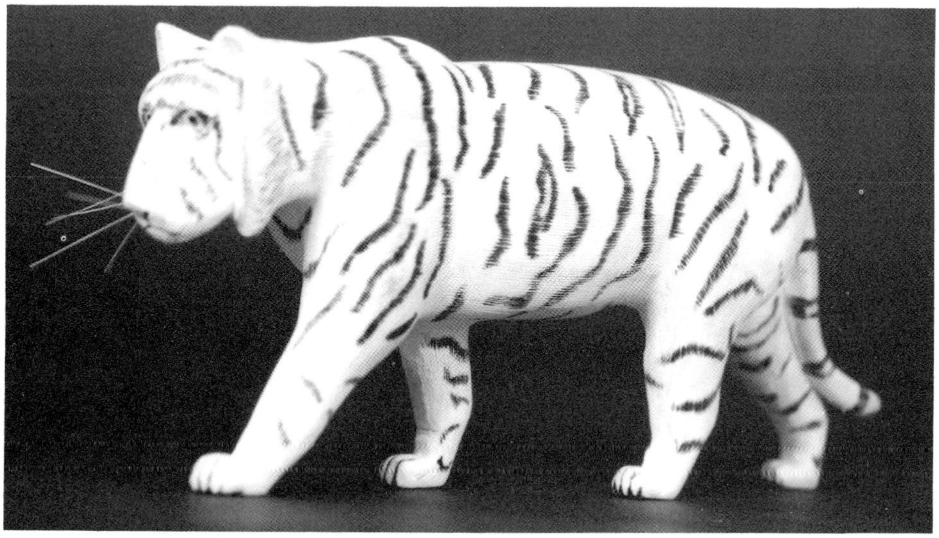

The detail on the left side showing the painting contrast between the white areas and tawny orange, and the whiskers. (See color figure 24).

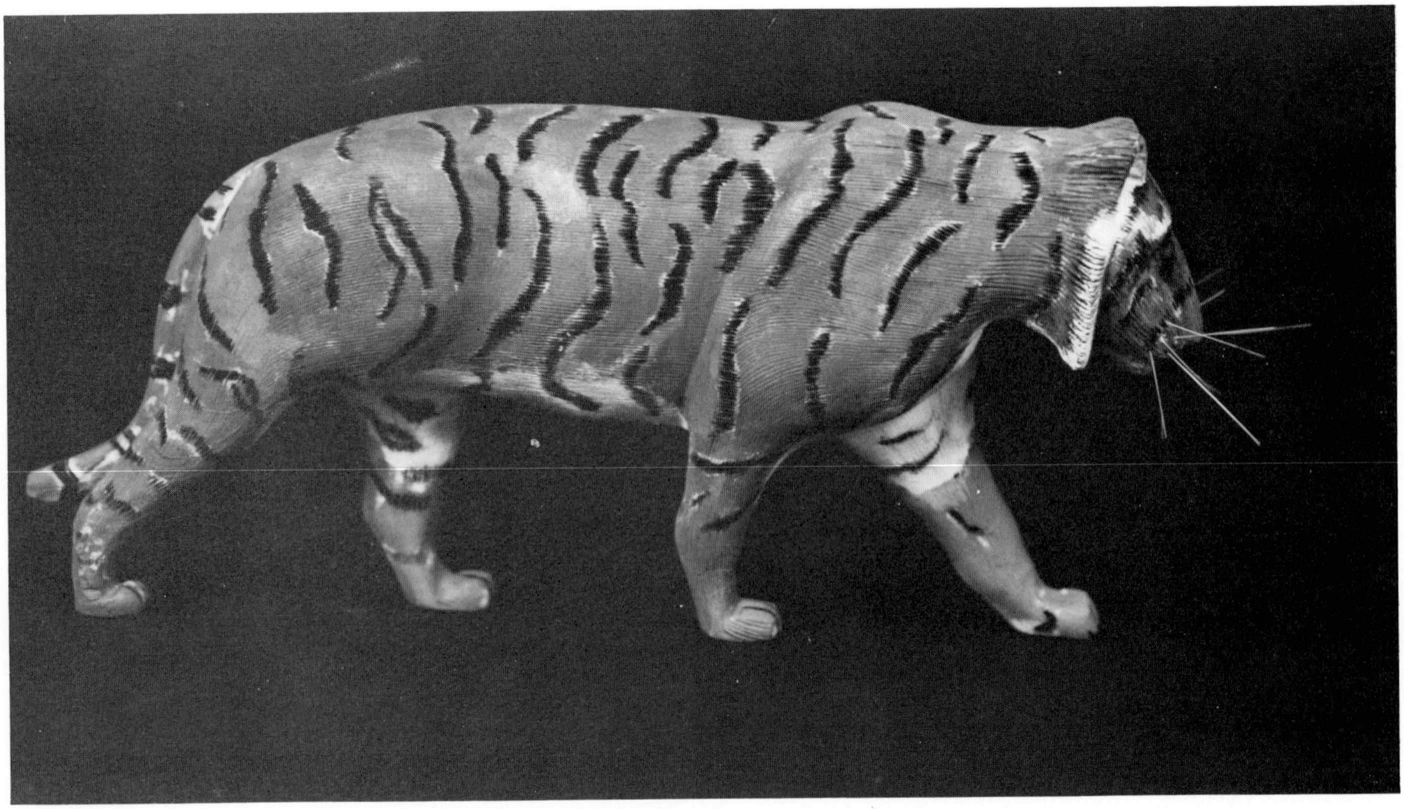

Figure 25 The right side of the tiger. Note the patch of white on the head. (See color figure 25).

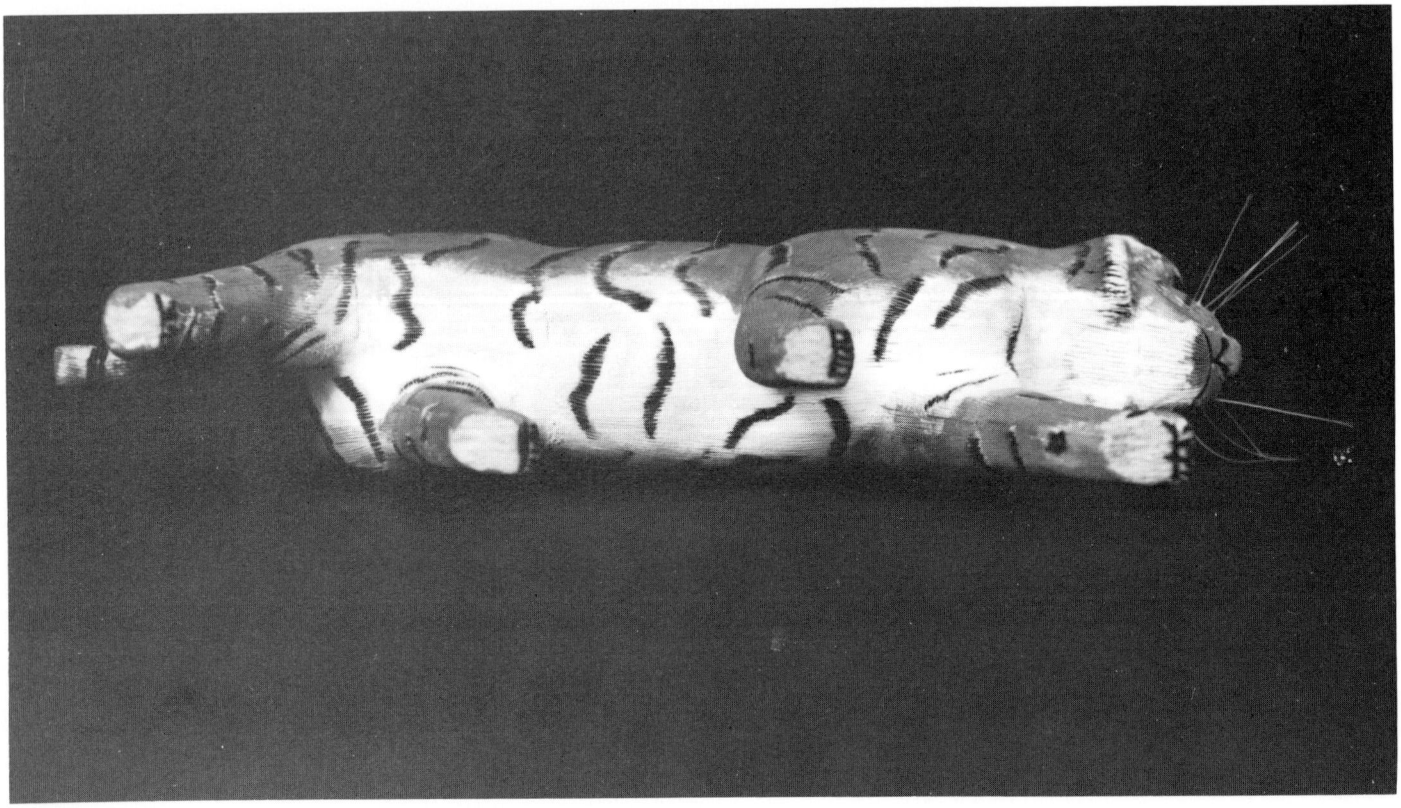

Figure 26 The underside of the tiger. (See color figure 26).

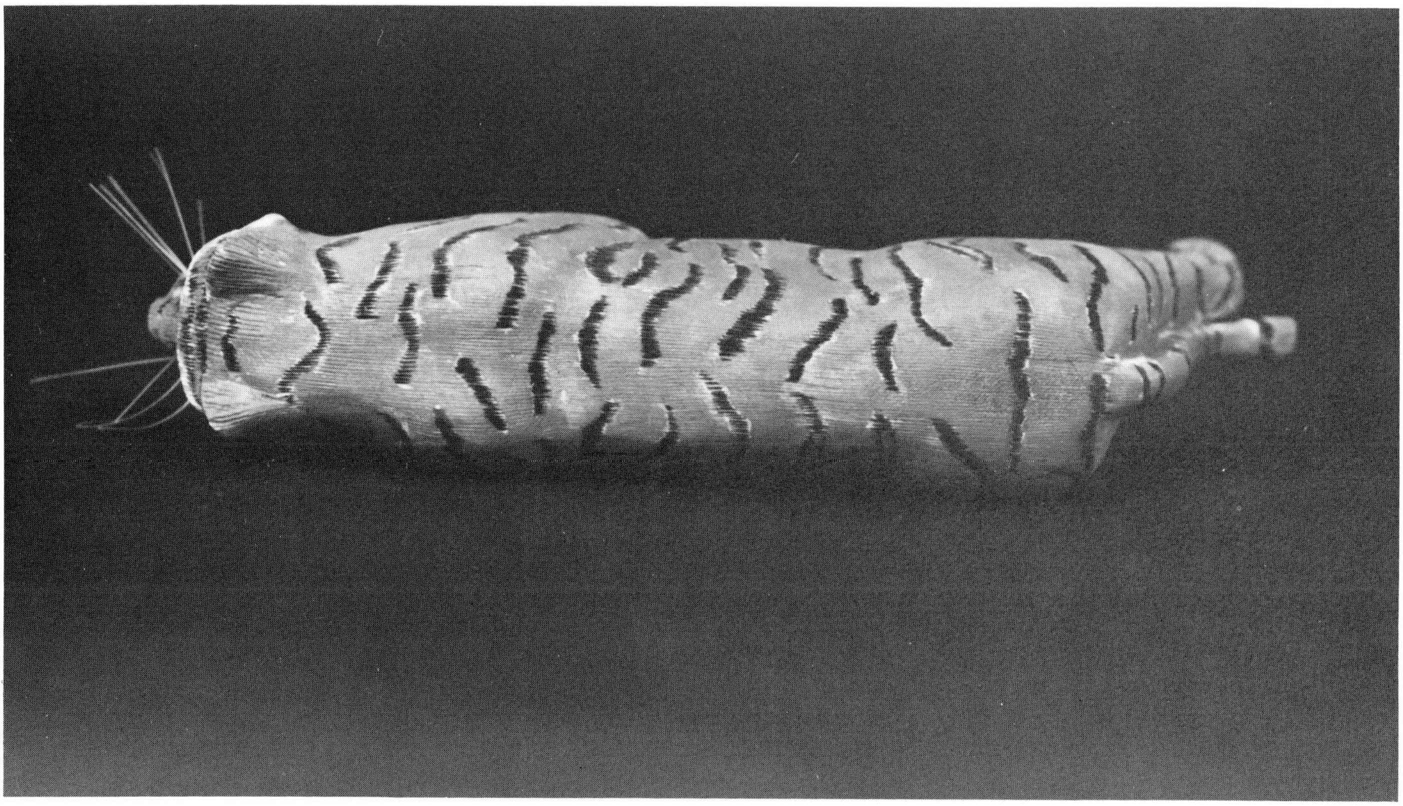

Figure 27 Top view of tiger. (See color figure 27).

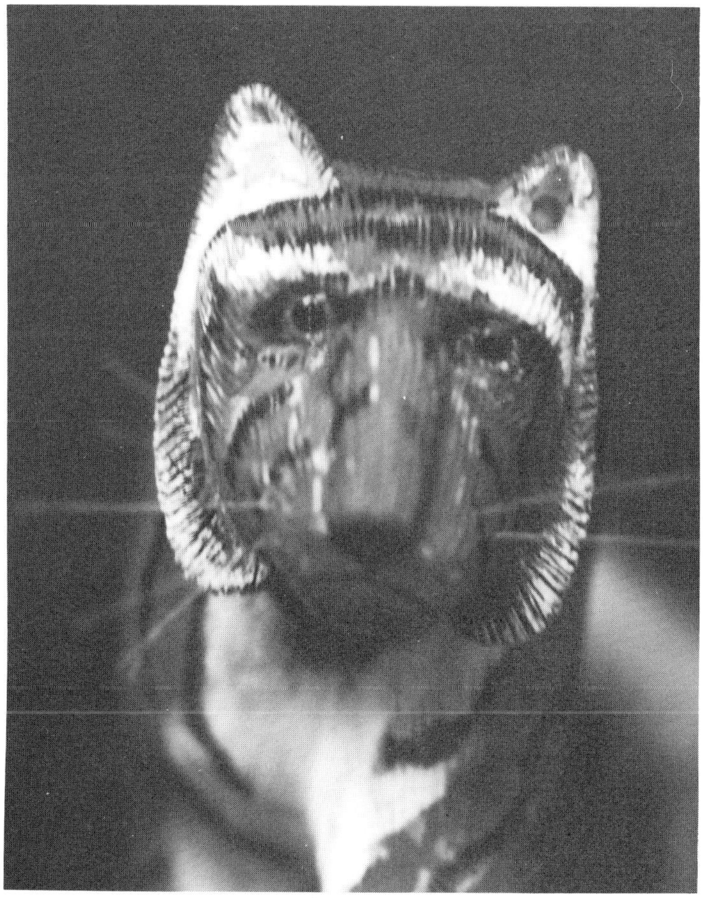

Figure 28

Front view of tiger. (See color figure 28).

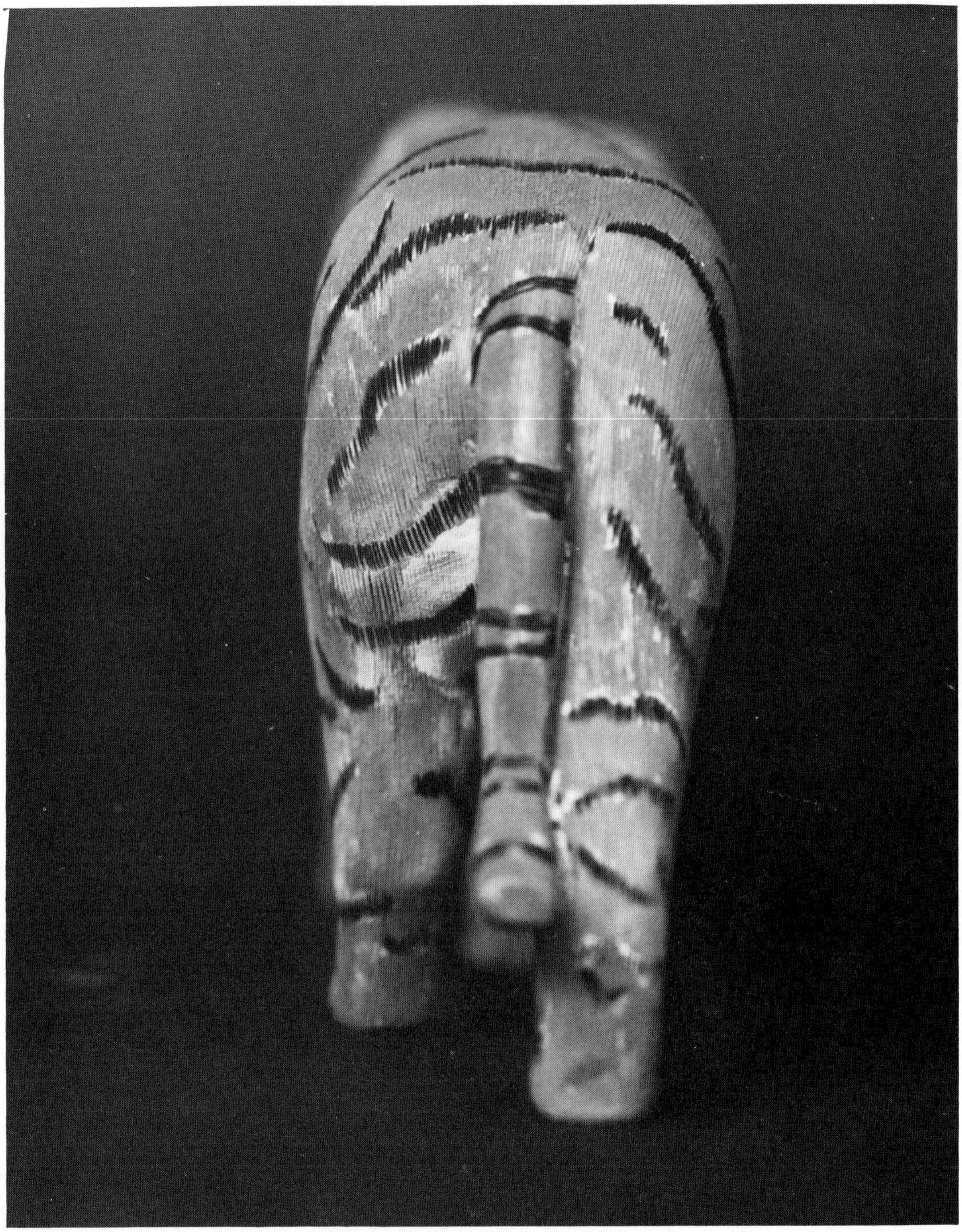

Figure 29

Rear view. (See color figure 29).

The American Goldfinch

Materials And Tools Needed

Basswood block 2" x 2" x 5"	Quick drying glue	Acrylic paint
2 mm glass eyes, clear	Dremel carving heads	Titanium white
Carving knives (X-acto)	1/8 inch drill, Nos. 125, 195 & 115	Cadmium yellow
Flexible shaft hobby tool	Drum sander	Medium Mars black
Burning pen with rheostat control	Paint Brushes Nos. 1 & 2	Brilliant orange
Epoxy putty	Sandpaper	Burnt Umber

The American Goldfinch is common in flocks in weedy fields, bushes, and seed bearing trees. It is fond of thistles, sunflowers, and dandelions. Our only other bright-yellow bird with black cap and wings is the much larger Evening Grosbeak. The male has a stubby finched bill, wing bars, notched tail, whitish rump, and rollercoaster flight. The canary yellow color is its summer coat. The song is long, high, and sweet. The call, per-chik-o-ree, is diagnostic of this species. Both sounds are given in flight.

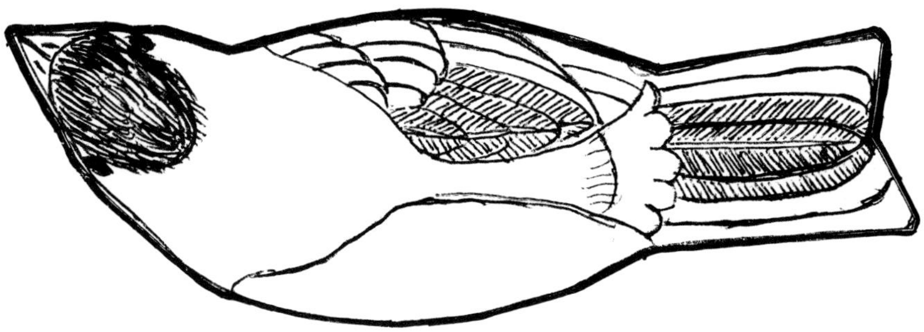

Figure 1

The top view of the Goldfinch with the sketch of the feather patterns. Note the tailfeathers, side wing feathers, and the limits of the black cap.

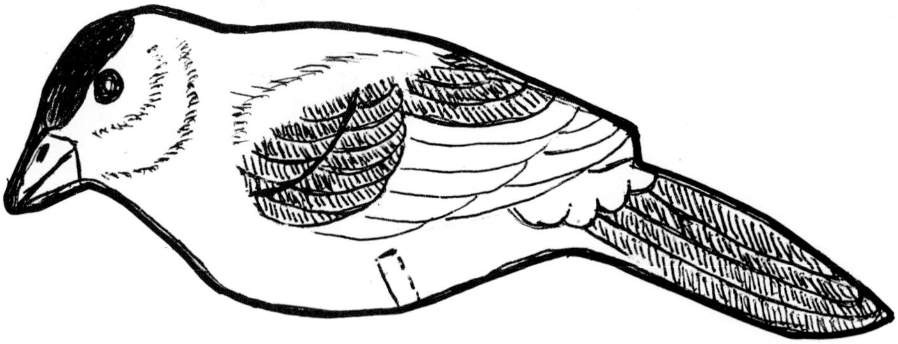

Figure 2

The side view pattern showing the sketching of the wing bars, the primaries, the upper tail coverts, and secondaries. This is commonly called the Topography of the bird. This is shown to aid your development of the carving.

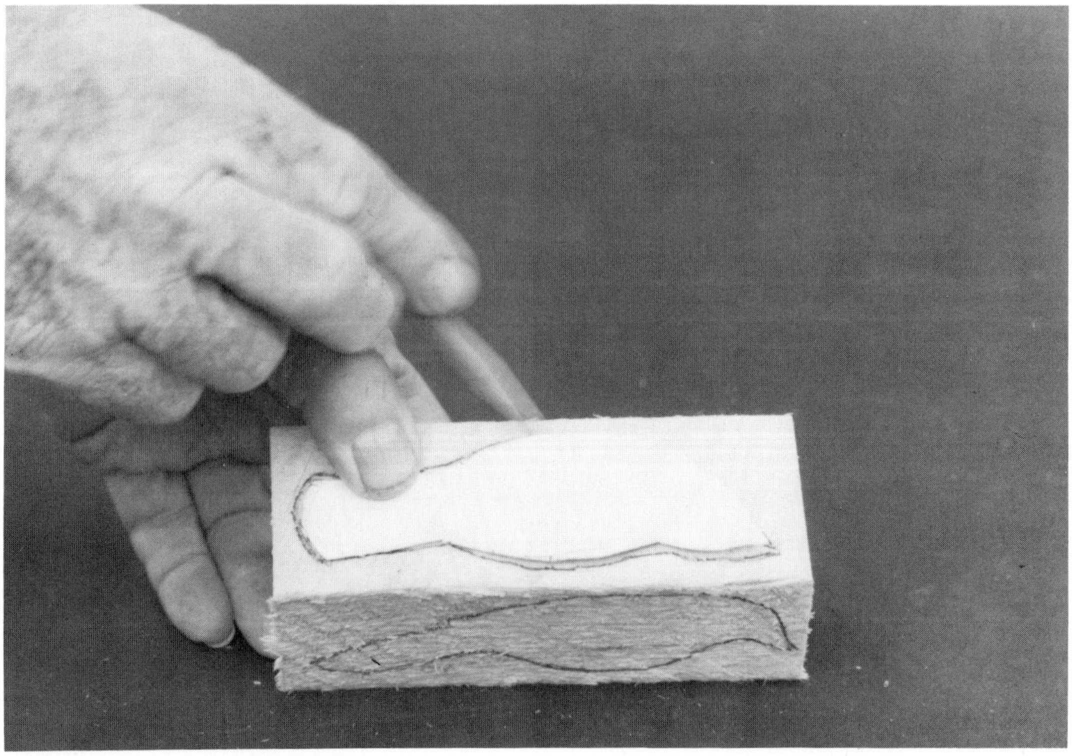

Figure 3

Tracing the top view on the 2" x 2" x 5" block of basswood.

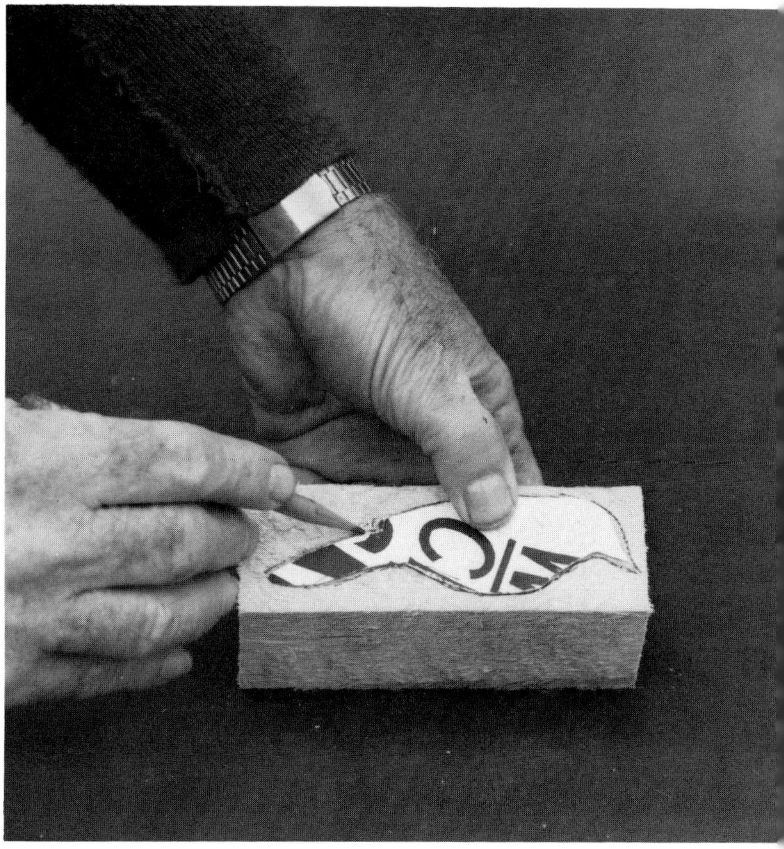

Figure 4

Tracing the side view on the wood.

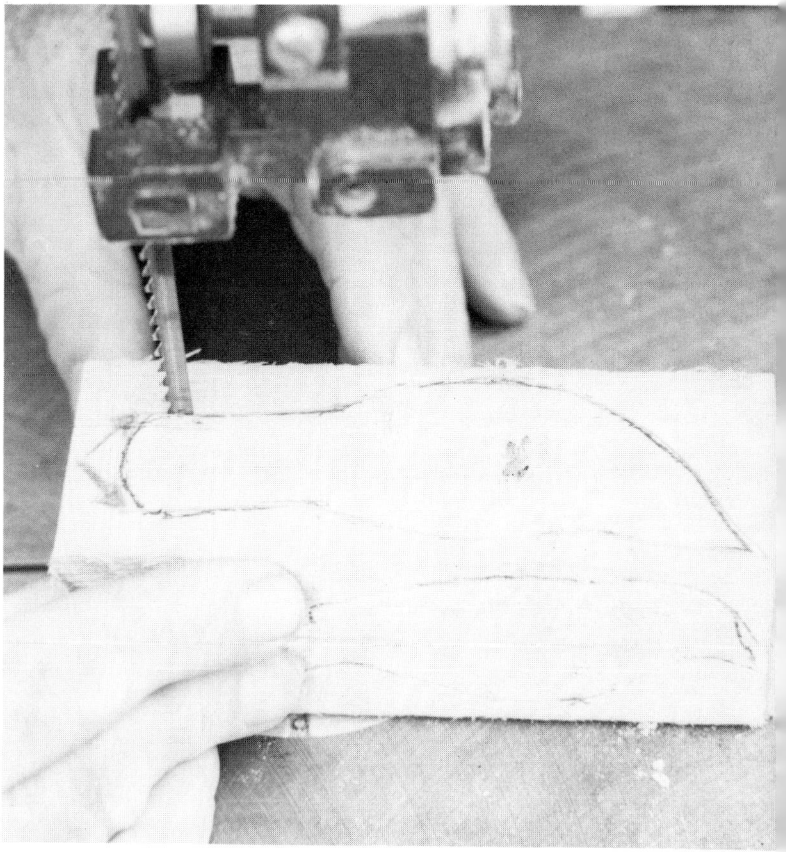

Figure 5

Cutting out the top view with the saw. Start to cut at the beak and stop cutting at the end of the tail. This will leave the block solid to cut out the side view.

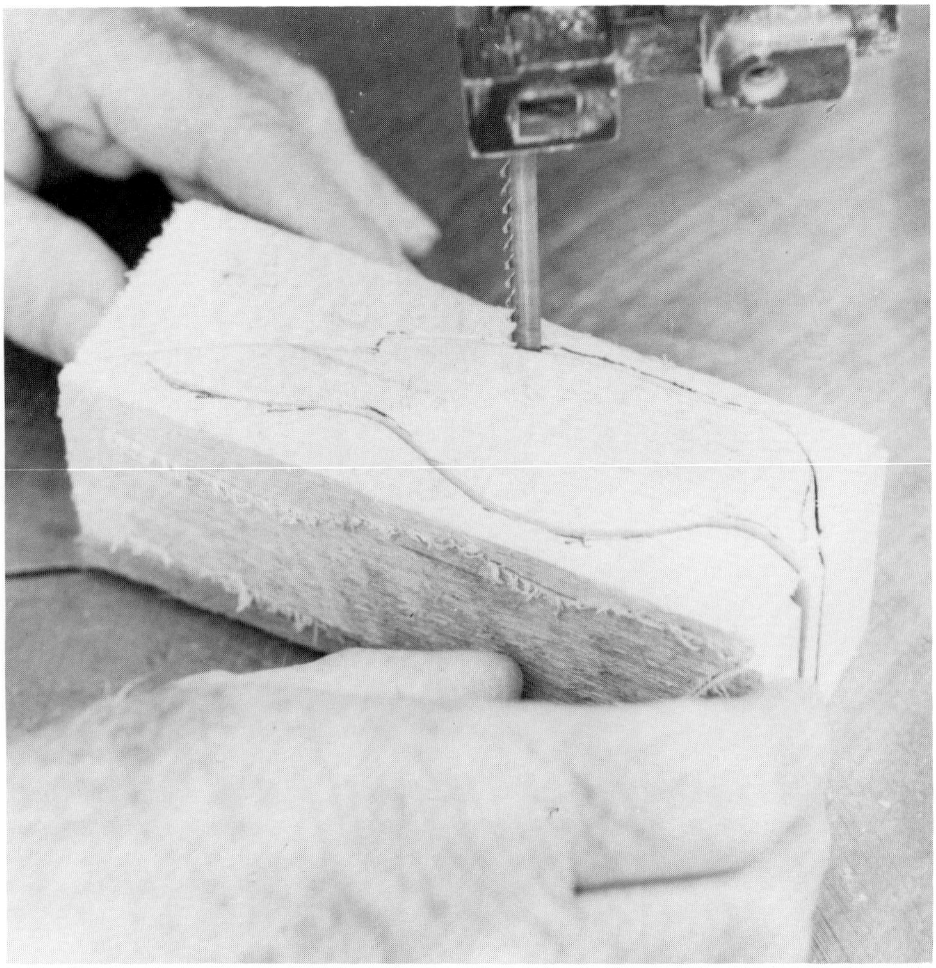

Figure 6

Cut out the side view completely with the saw as shown. Again, start to cut at the beak end.

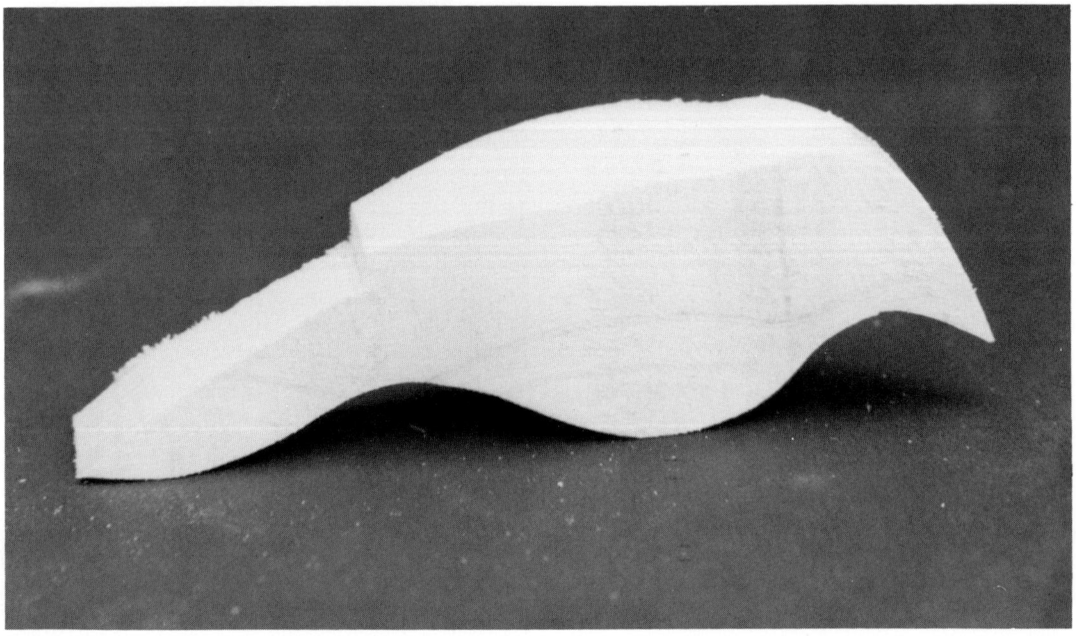

Figure 7

The Goldfinch ready to carve. (Side view)

Figure 8

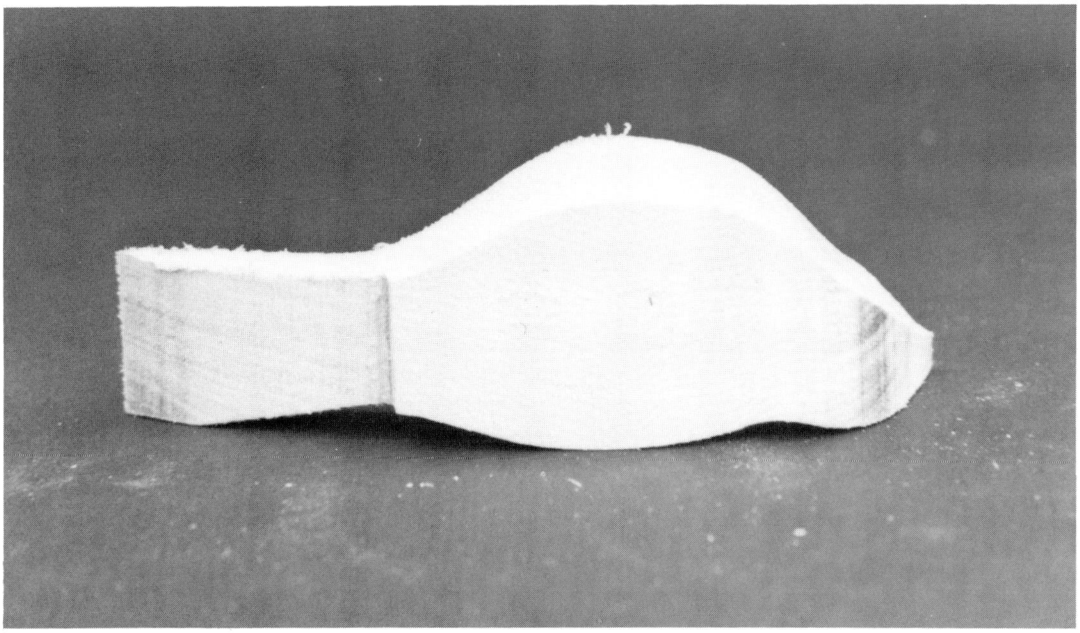

The top view of the cut out. Note the position of the head to give a natural look!

The bird is carved with X-acto knives and a flexible shaft hobby tool. The X-acto knives are inexpensive and the interchangeable variety of blades permit the carver to develop difficult areas in the carving.

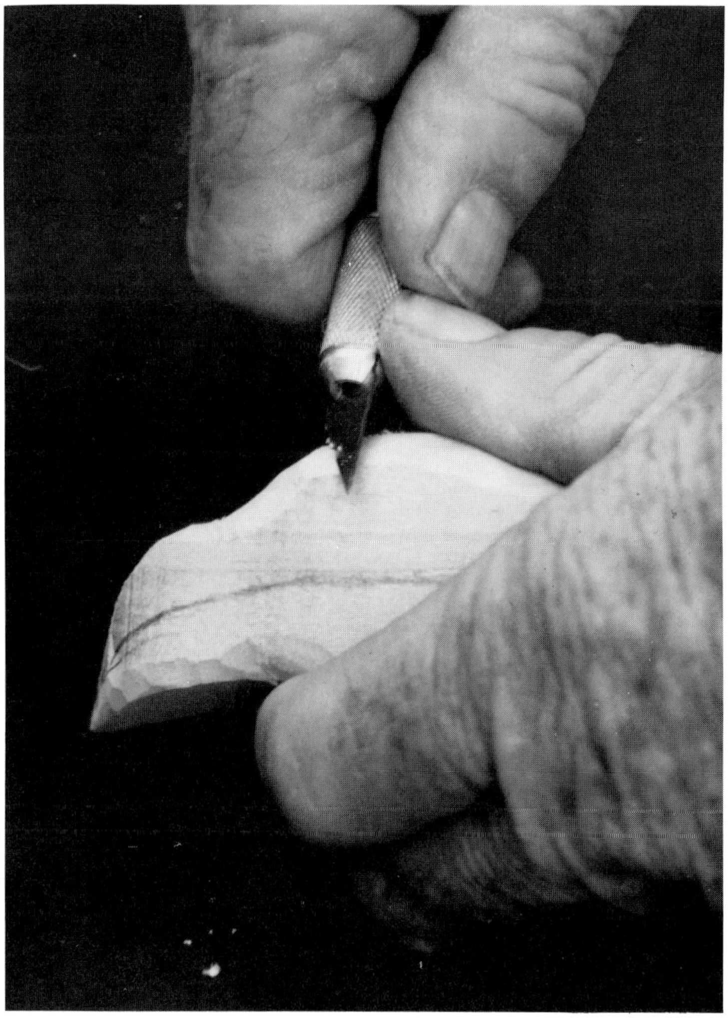

Figure 9

This is the carving technique which is the safest. The straight-bladed knife is held in the right hand and the power or the thrust is made with the left thumb placed on the handle of the knife near the blade. Taking small chips one at a time can save time, prevent error, and permit the safest procedure. Practice this method until it becomes comfortable for you.

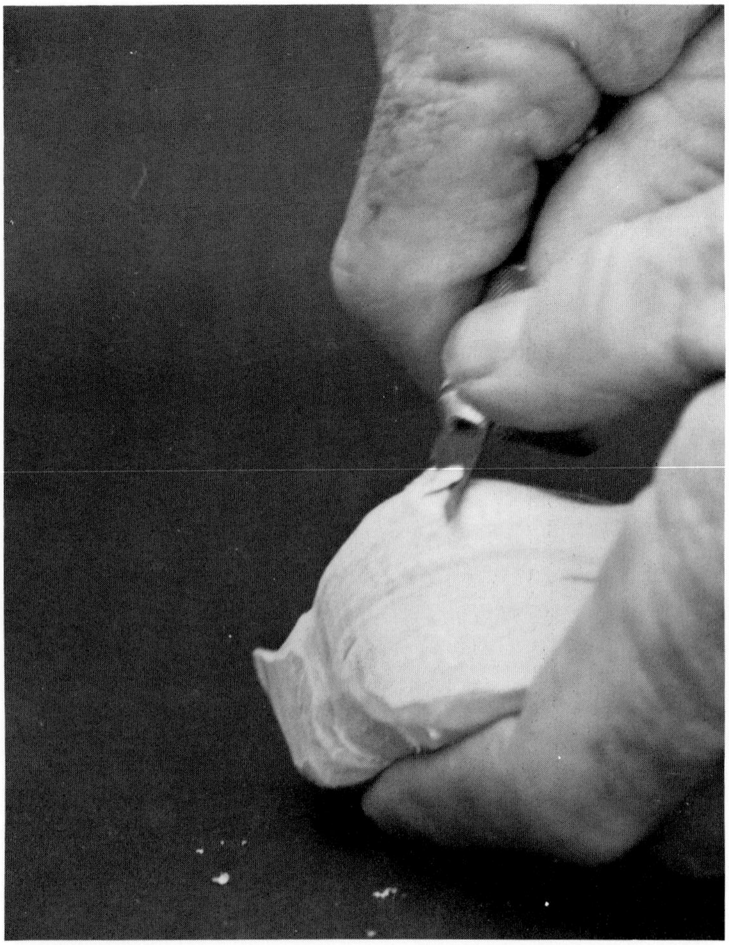

Figure 10

The knife is used to round out the body of the bird. This rounding out procedure is continued throughout. The head is shaped and the square corners on the tail are rounded and cut back to a thickness of 1/8 inch.

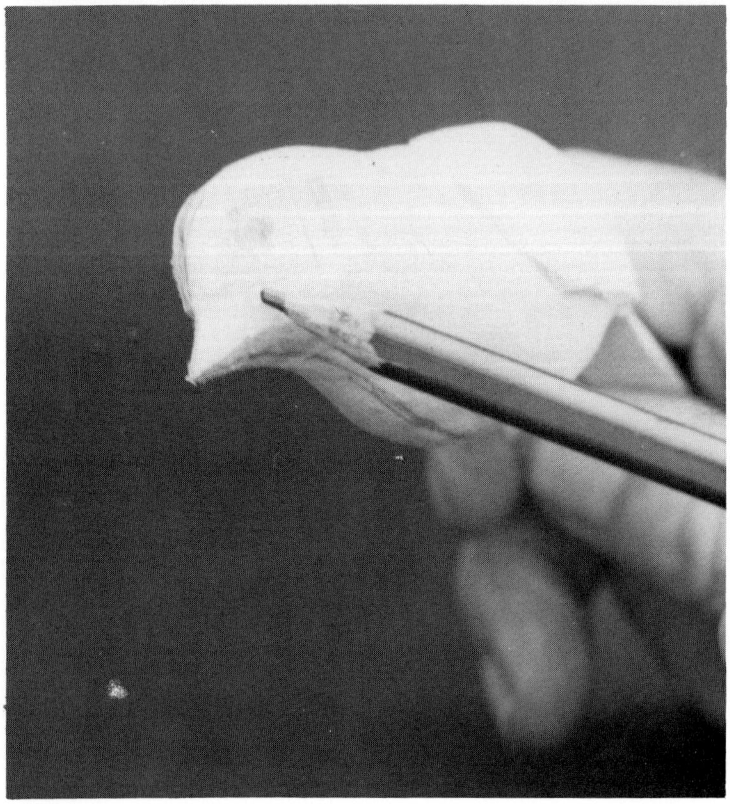

Figure 11

The beak after the steps to round the head and locate the eye socket. Insert a small hole in your pattern at the center of the eye and trace the location of it on both sides of the head.

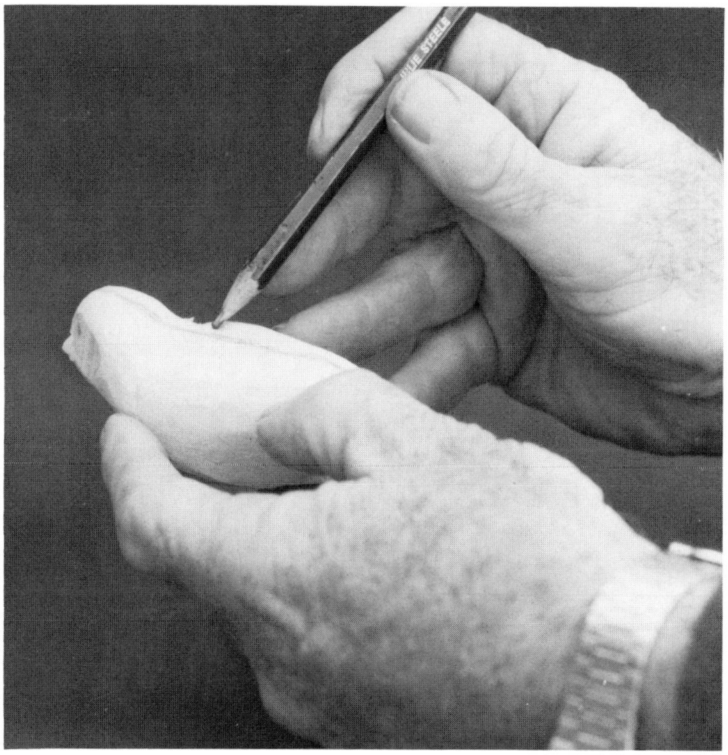

Figure 12

The bird has now been shaped and all sharp corners rounded. Initial sanding has been completed using a hobby tool equipped with a drum sander and a fine grit band. The entire bird can now be hand sanded.

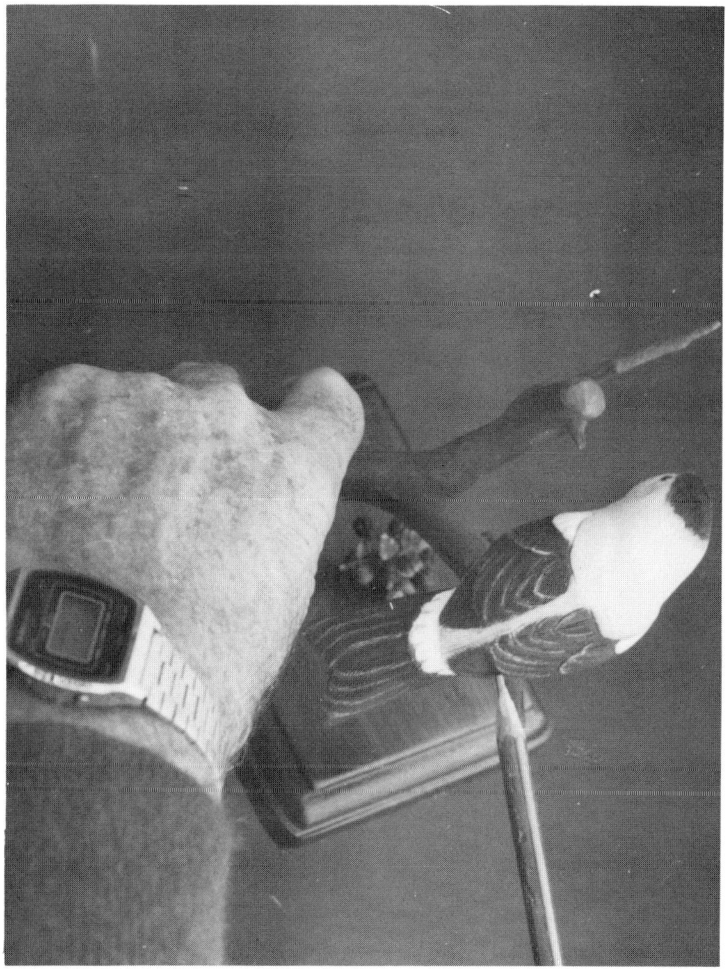

Figure 13

The carving detail of the side wings, shoulders, rump, and tail are shown. Note the V-shaped tail, the separation between the side wings, and shoulder structure.

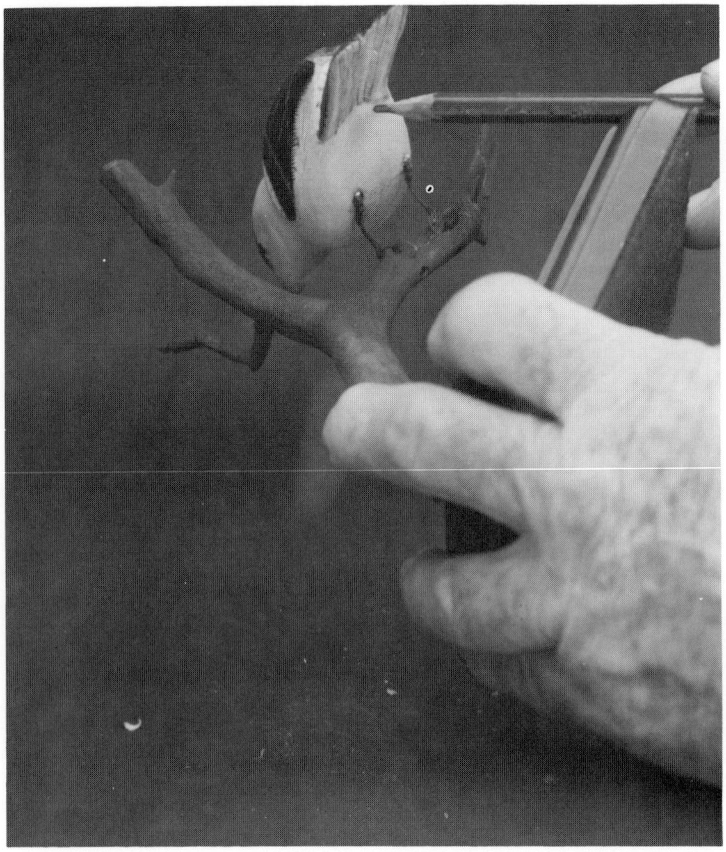

Figure 14

The underneath detail of the rump and hips for inserting the legs.

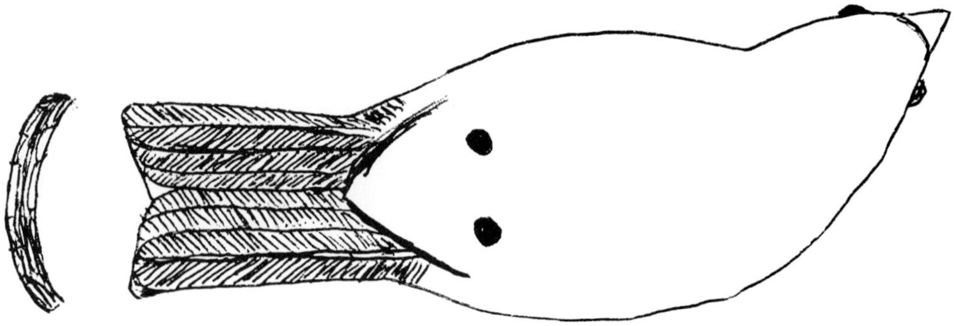

Figure 15

Detail of underneath.

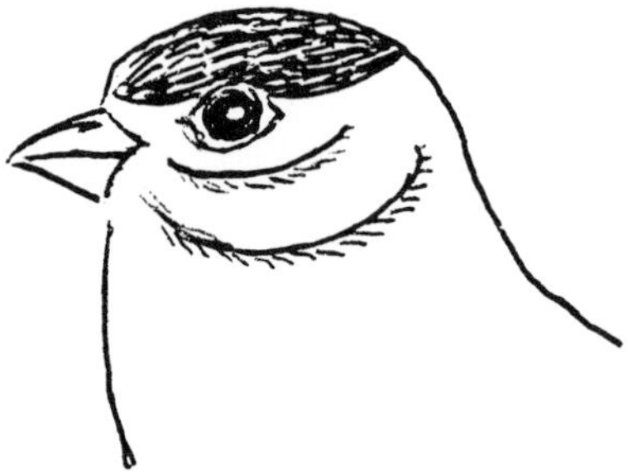

Detail of head.

The sketches in figure 15 show details of tailfeathers and the area to carve in the rump underneath. The location to drill 1/8" holes for the legs is shown. The details that are prominent on the head are the beak, the eye ring and the cheek line. All of these lines when carved will add realism to your bird.

The cross-section of the tail is also shown with 1/8 inch thickness.

Figure 16

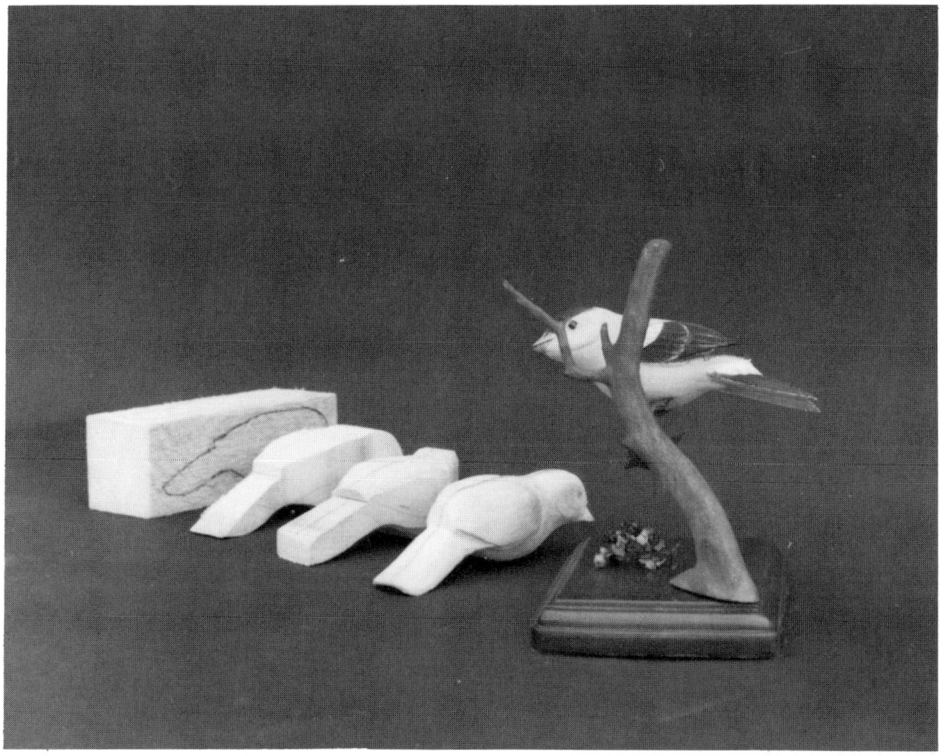

The five basic steps of carving from the wooden block to the mounted Goldfinch. The fourth step shows the eye sockets drilled using moto-tool cutting head number 125. The carving is then sanded with medium sandpaper, bathed in alcohol and then sanded with fine sandpaper.

The next step involves texturing with a burning pen equipped with a rheostat. Figures 1 and 2 show the feather patterns. Outline the patterns on your carving with a pencil, and burn the wing feathers, tail feathers, and top notch with dark burn. The remainder of the feathers are textured with a light burn. This will aid with the painting steps.

Using 2 millimeter glass eyes which have been painted dark brown, insert the eyes in the sockets. First fill the sockets with epoxy putty so that they are level full. Shape a lid with the excess putty and let it set overnight.

Using a 1/8 inch drill, make the holes to insert the Goldfinch legs. The legs can be obtained from a supplier who pours hot lead into molds for birds' feet and legs.

Do not glue the legs and feet in place until the last step before mounting your bird. Paint the legs using acrylic burnt umber.

On the carving, using a stiff brush, briskly brush away the char left by the burning process so as not to dirty the paint.

Spray clear acrylic protective coating on the bird and let it dry.

Using mars black, paint the top of the tail, the wings, and the top notch.

Using titanium white with a slight touch of raw sienna, paint the rump area and the wing feathers near the shoulder.

Using a #00 brush, paint the tips of the secondary wing feathers with a slight white edge.

Mix white and mars black and paint the tail underneath a light gray.

The rest of your Goldfinch is painted with the yellow acrylic paint.

After each painting step dry the carving with a hair dryer. Some areas may require two or three coats of paint.

Glue in the legs and select a mounting of your choice as shown in figure 17. The seed structure on the pine base is bitter sweet.

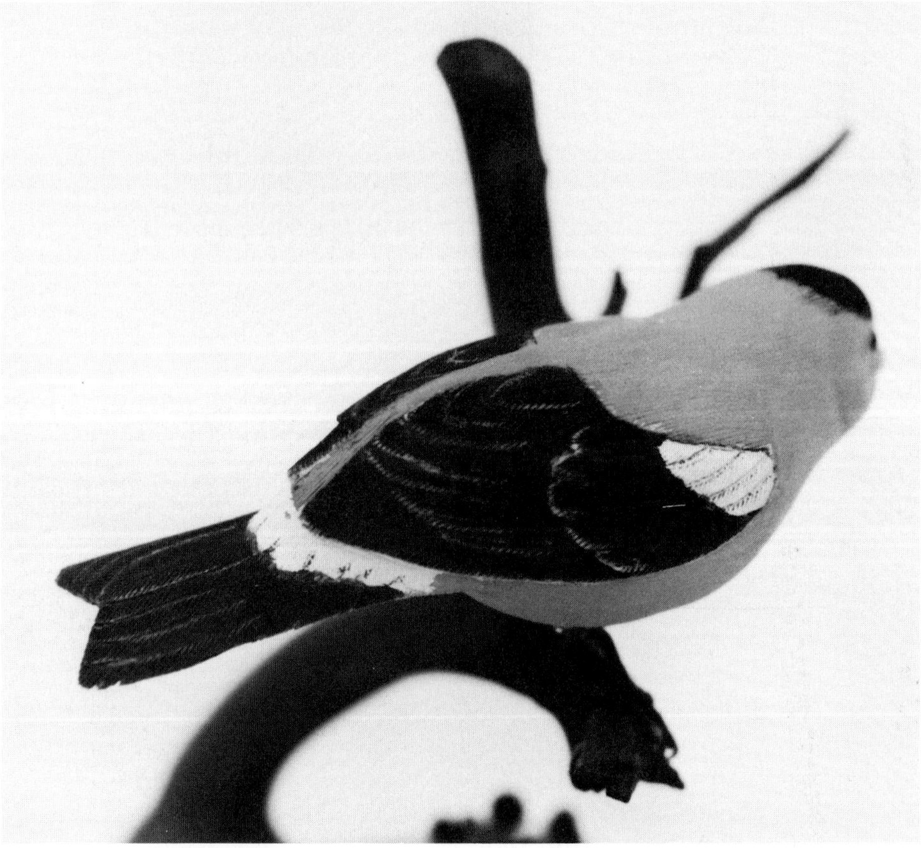

Figure 17

Side view of the Goldfinch on a tree branch. Note the painting of the rump, tail, and side wing feathers. (See color figure 17).

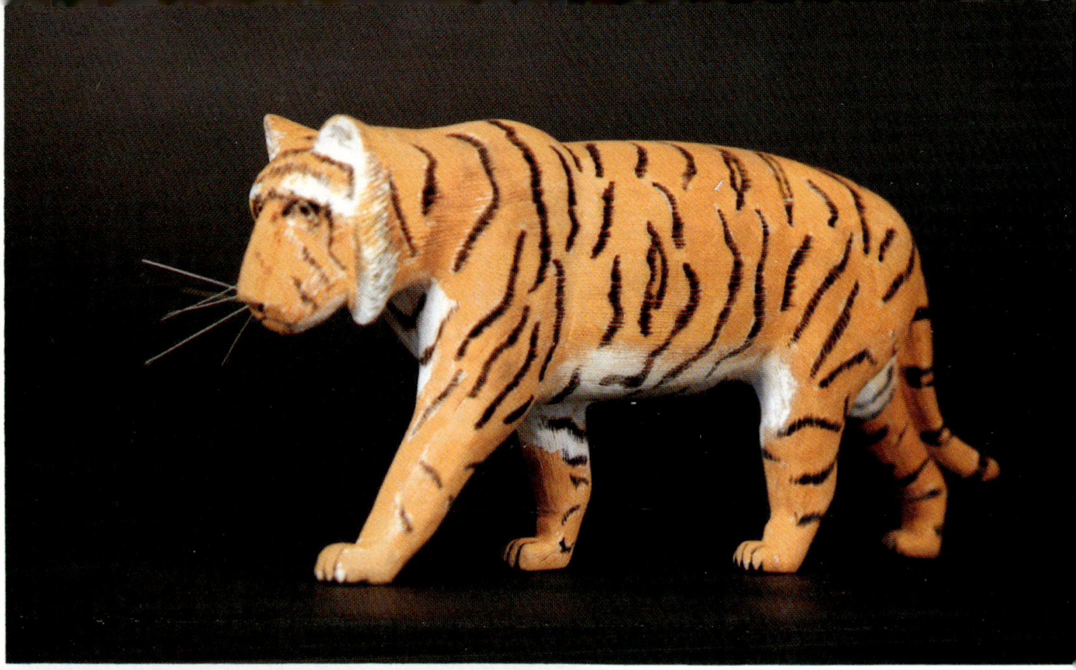

Tiger color figure 24.

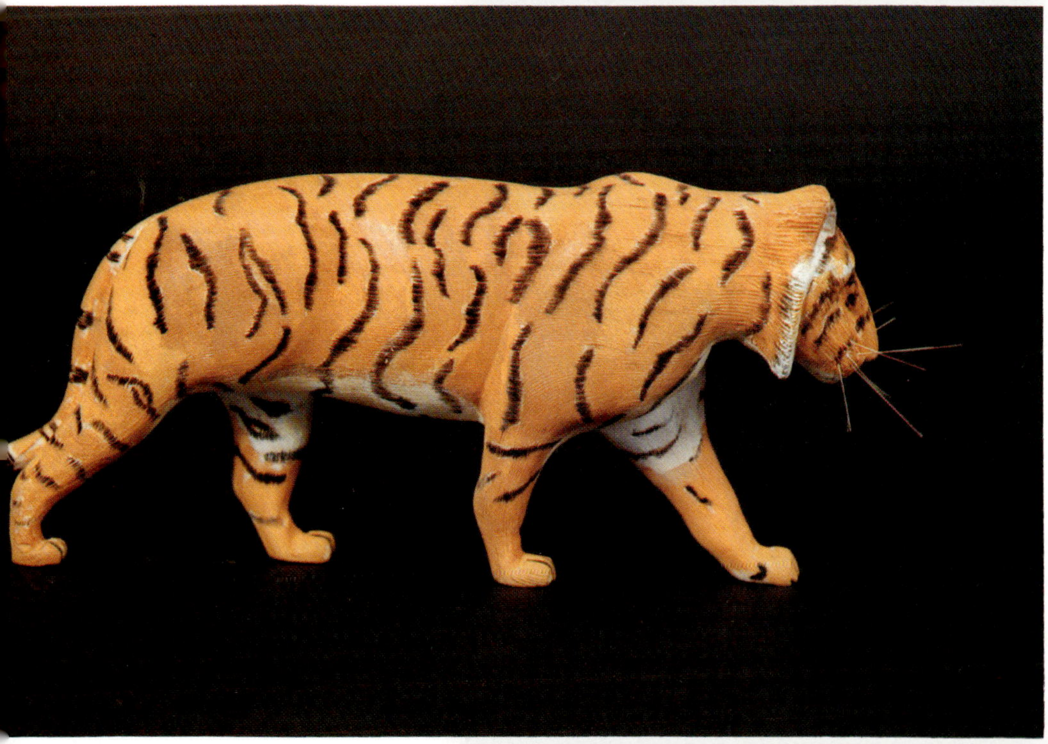

Tiger color figure 25.

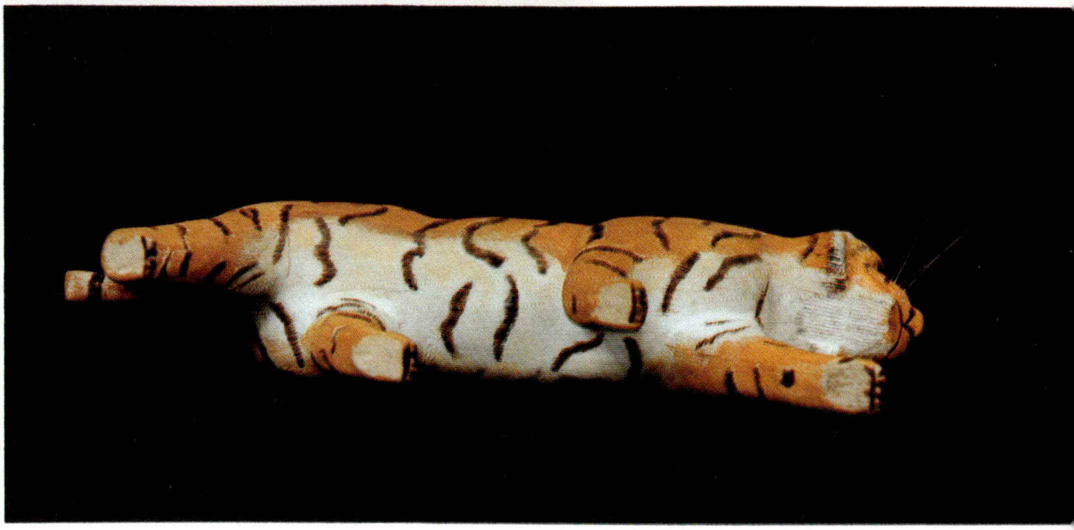

Tiger color figure 26.

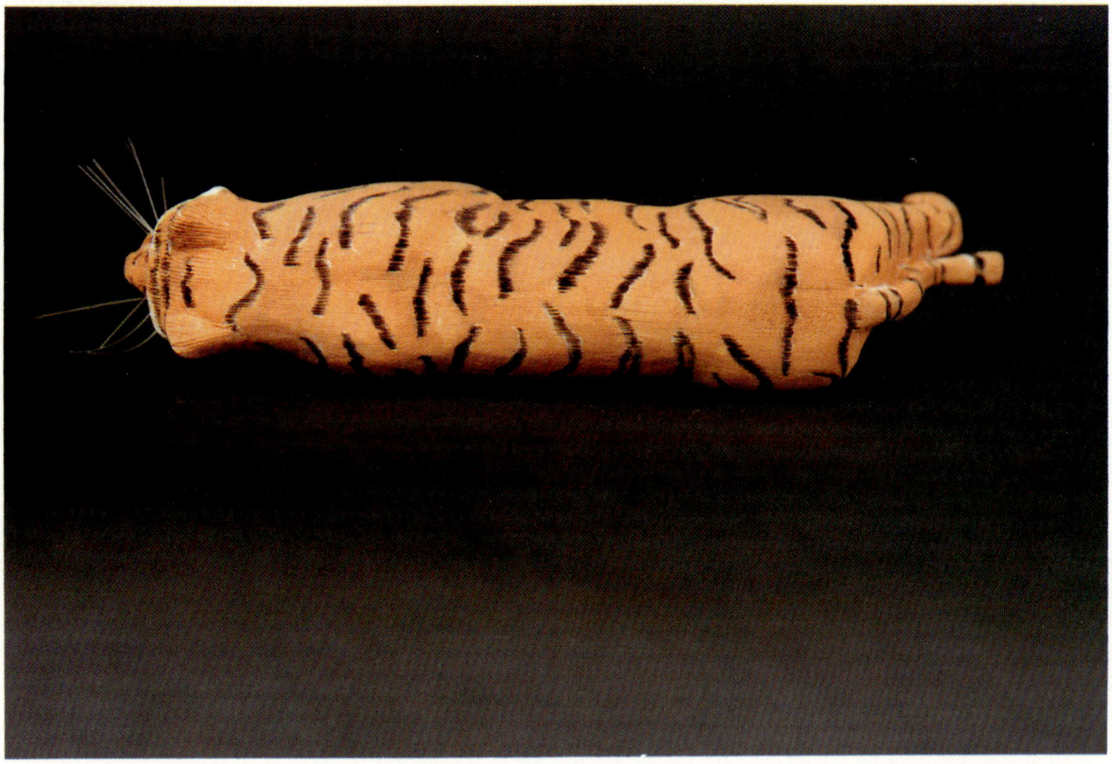

Tiger color figure 27.

Tiger color figure 28.

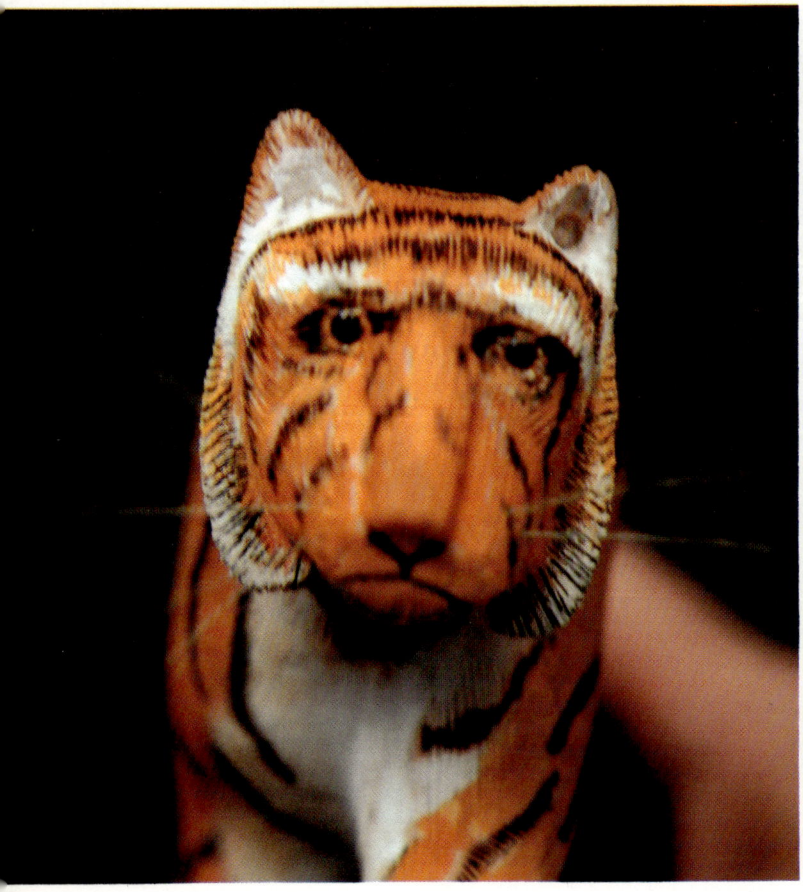

Tiger color figure 29.

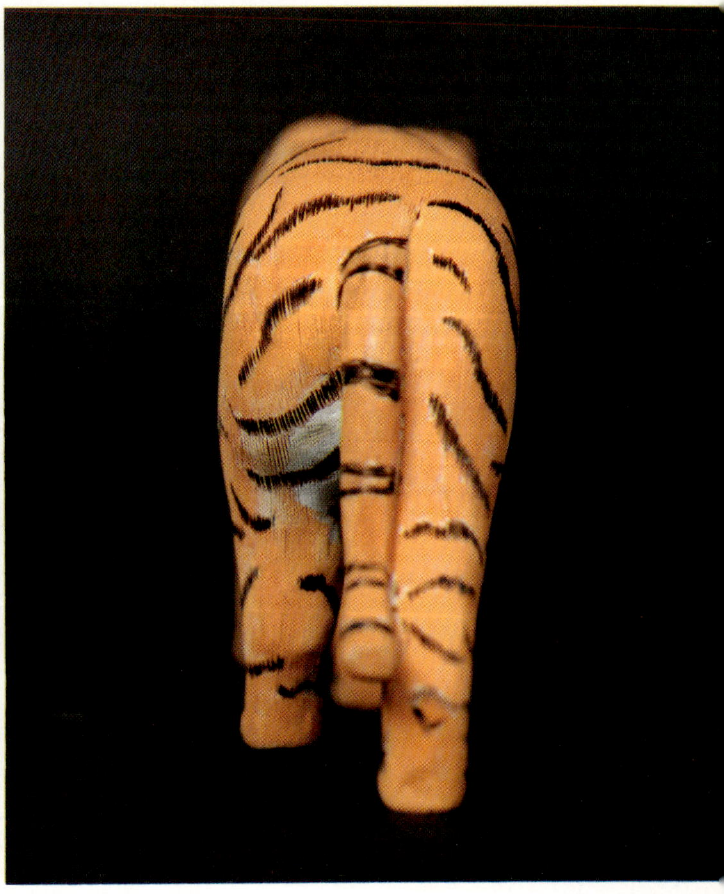

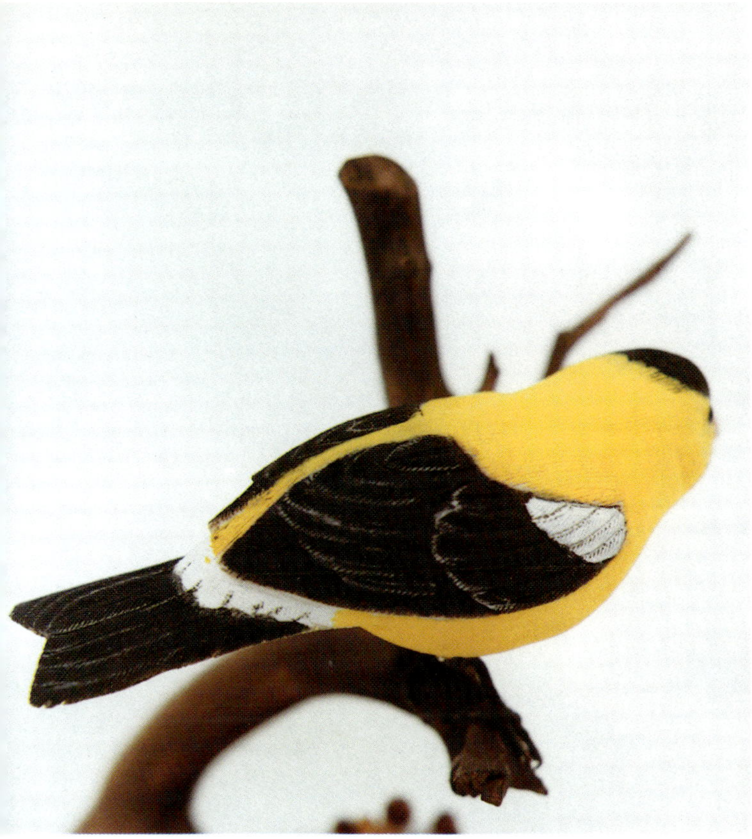

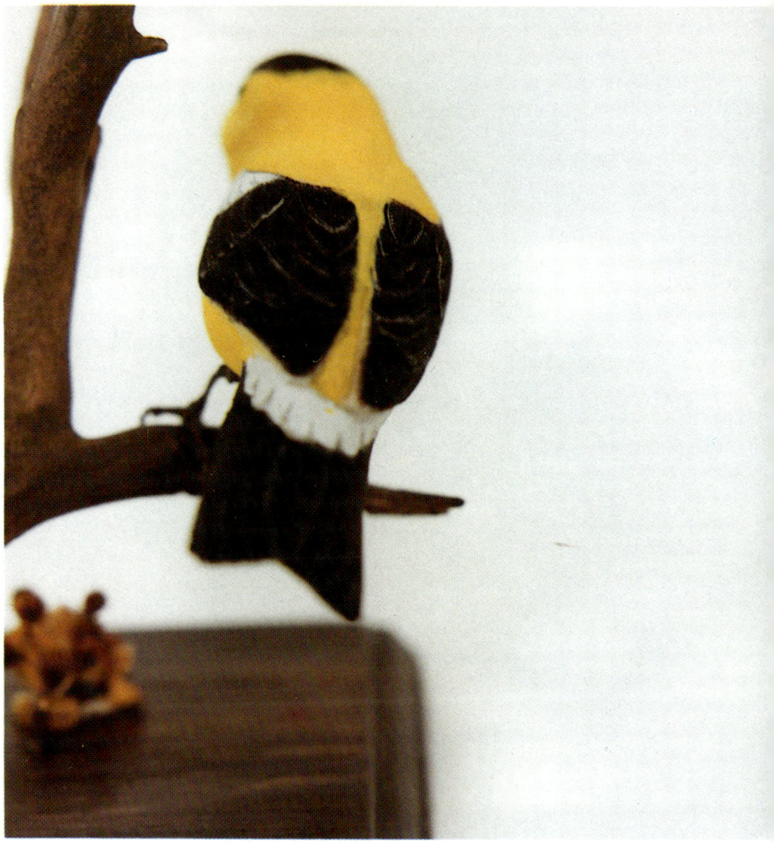

American Goldfinch color figure 17.

American Goldfinch color figure 18.

American Goldfinch color figure 19.

American Goldfinch color figure 20.

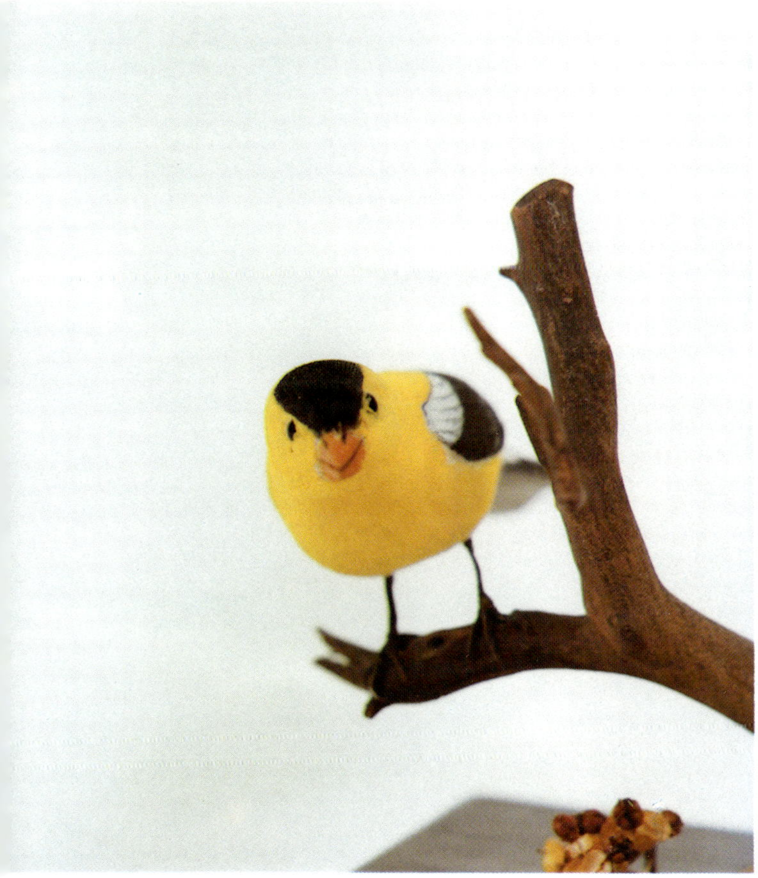

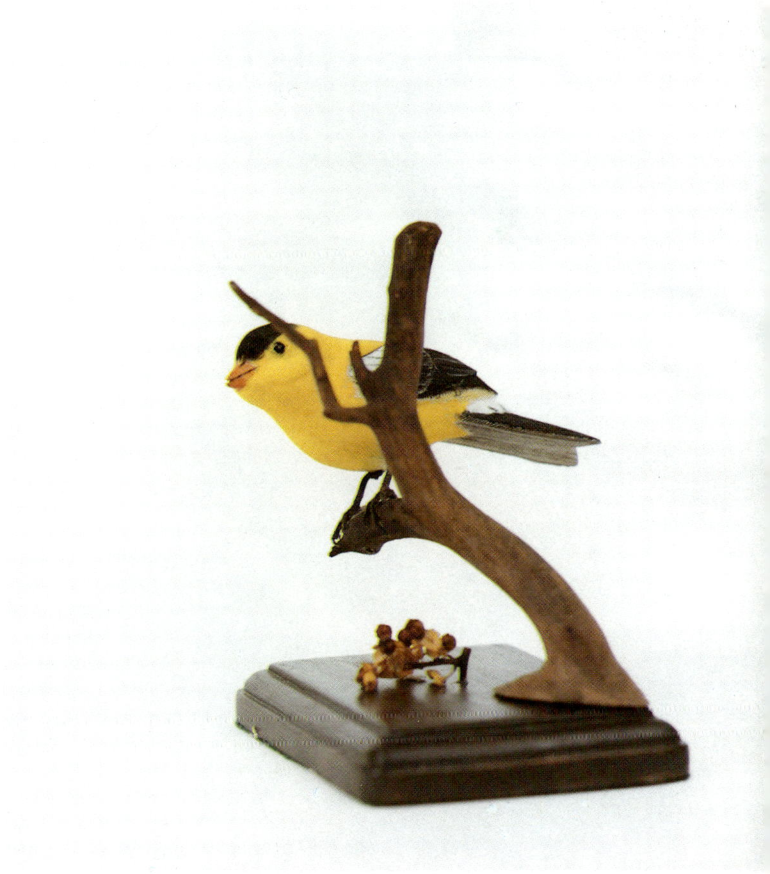

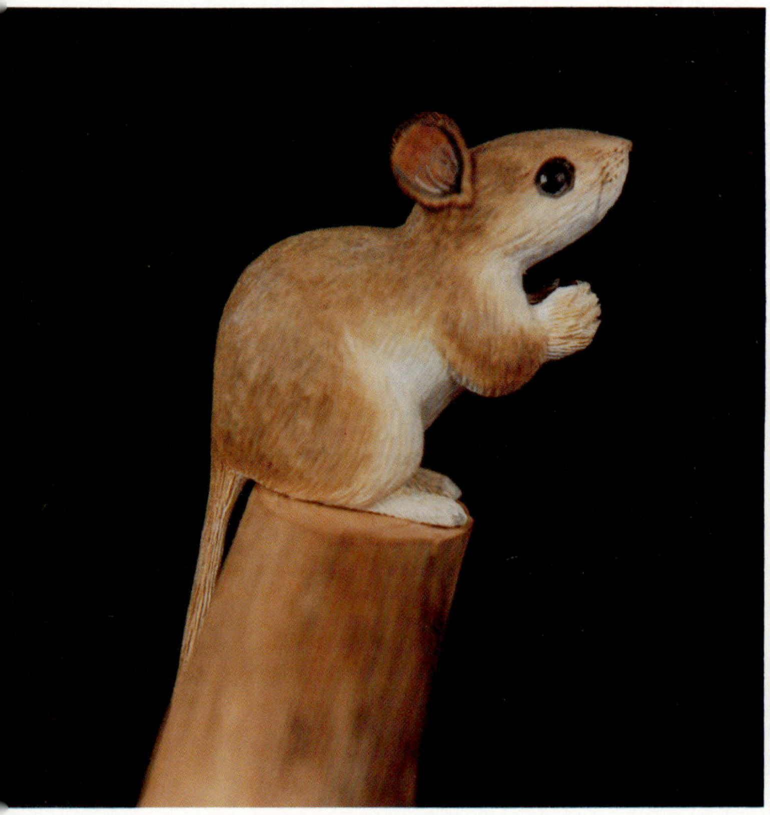

Mouse color figure 18.

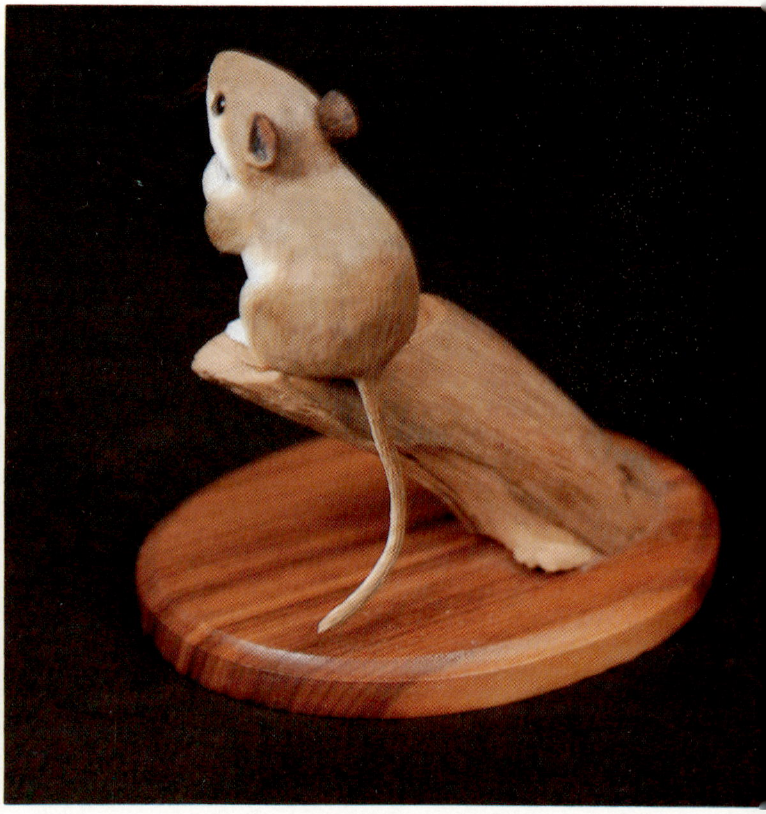

Mouse color figure 19.

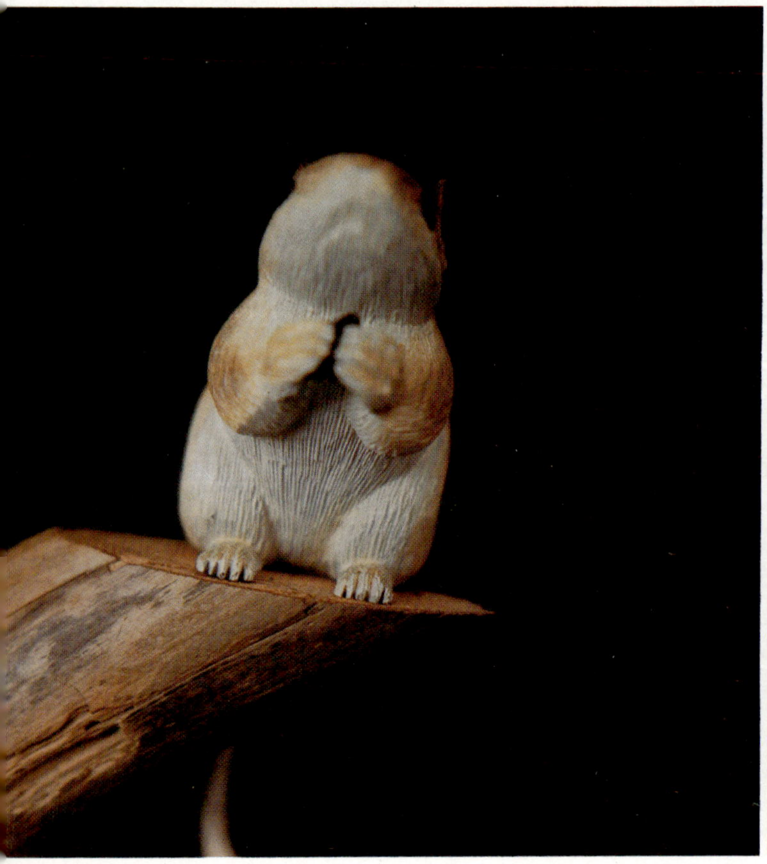

Mouse color figure 20.

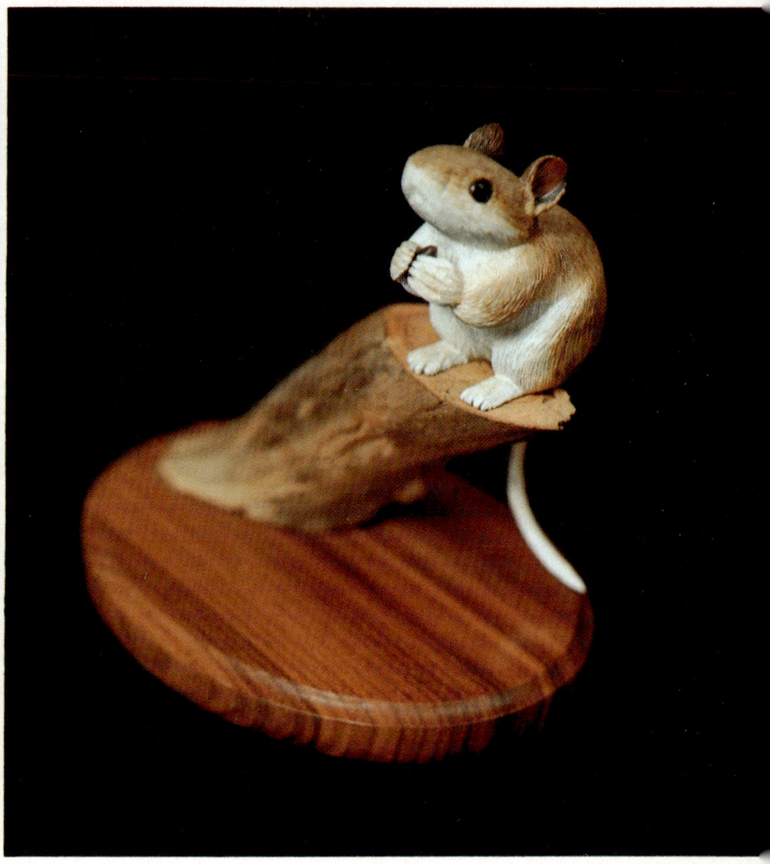

Mouse color figure 21.

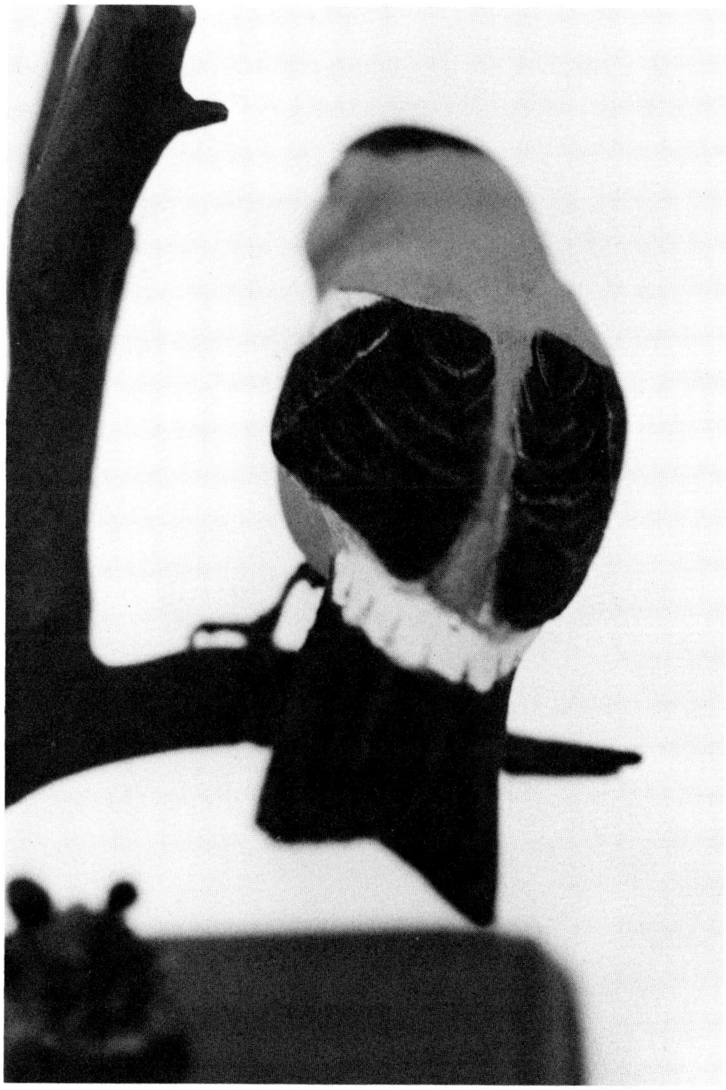

Figure 18

Back view. (See color figure 18).

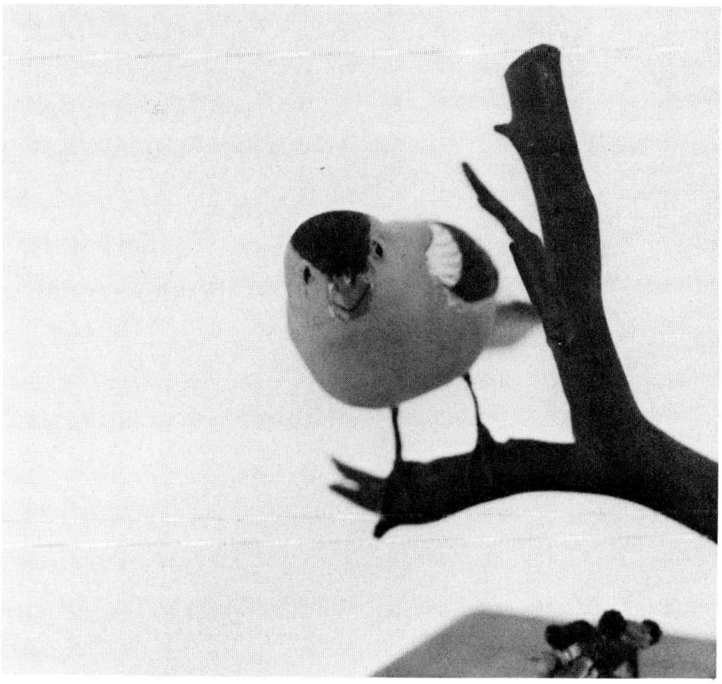

Figure 19

Front view. (See color figure 19).

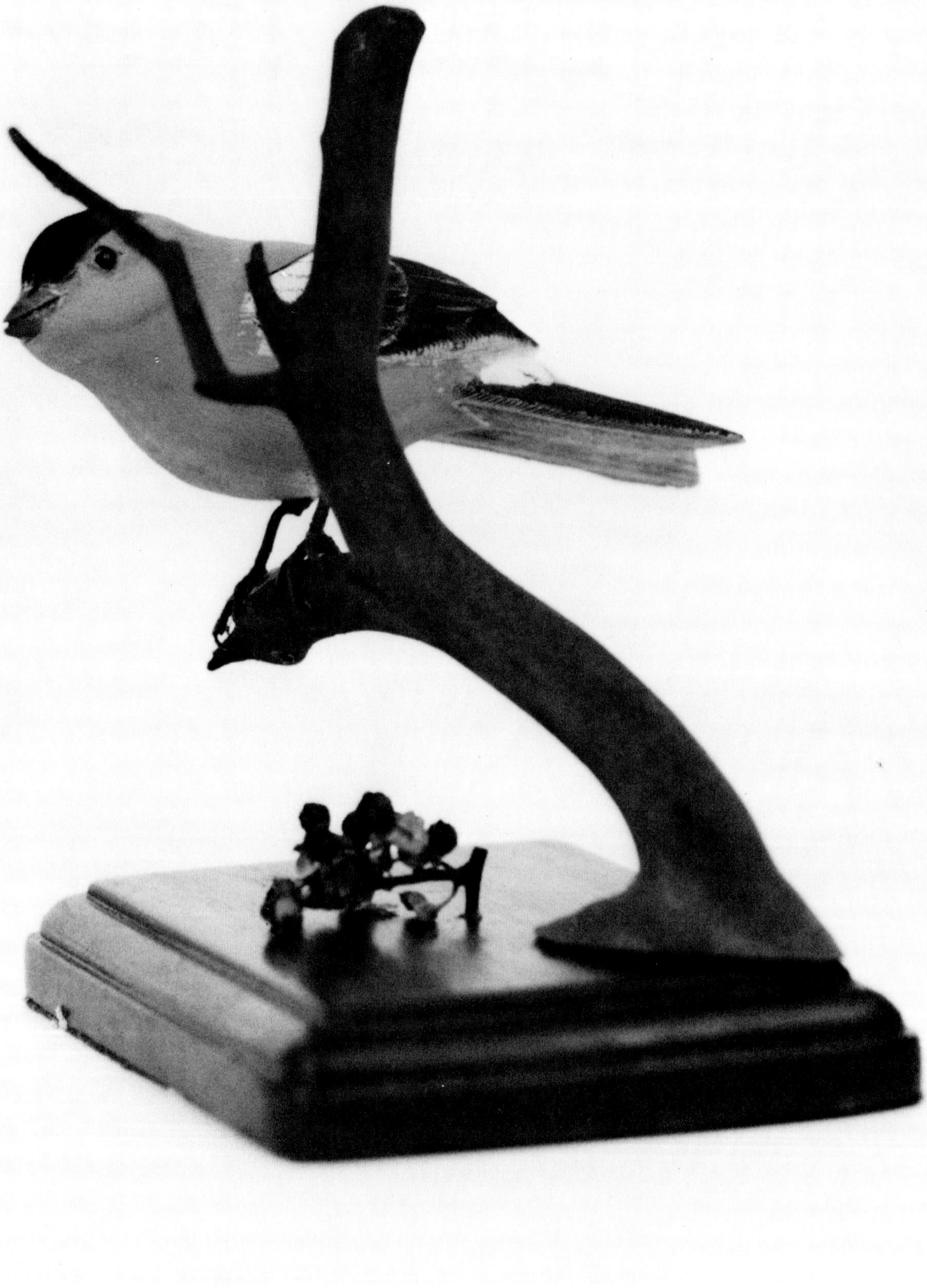

Figure 20

The Goldfinch mounted on a branch from a birch tree. The base is white pine with a twig of bittersweet to enhance the carving. Always place a felt cloth on the bottom of the base. (See color figure 20).

The Wood Mouse

Materials And Tools Needed

Basswood block 2" x 2" x 6"
Carving knives
Moto-tool
Dremel carving heads
Drum Sander. Nos. 115, 125 & 194

3 mm clear glass eyes
Epoxy putty
Paint brushes Nos. 0, 1, & 2
Sandpaper
Rubbing alcohol

Acrylic paint
- White
- Burnt Umber
- Raw Sienna
- Black

Mice are rodents, or gnawing animals. They have followed man to all parts of the globe. These animals have large eyes and ears, long whiskers, and are all suited for exploration at night. Their color is gray to grayish tan.

The wood mouse *(Muridae sylvaticus)* lives outdoors and has many bird and mammal enemies such as hawks, owls, crows, coyotes, foxes and skunks. Snakes also prey on mice. All of these enemies help to keep down the number of mice.

Using the pattern shown in figure 1, cut out the body using a jigsaw, bandsaw, or coping saw from a 2" x 2" x 6" block of basswood.

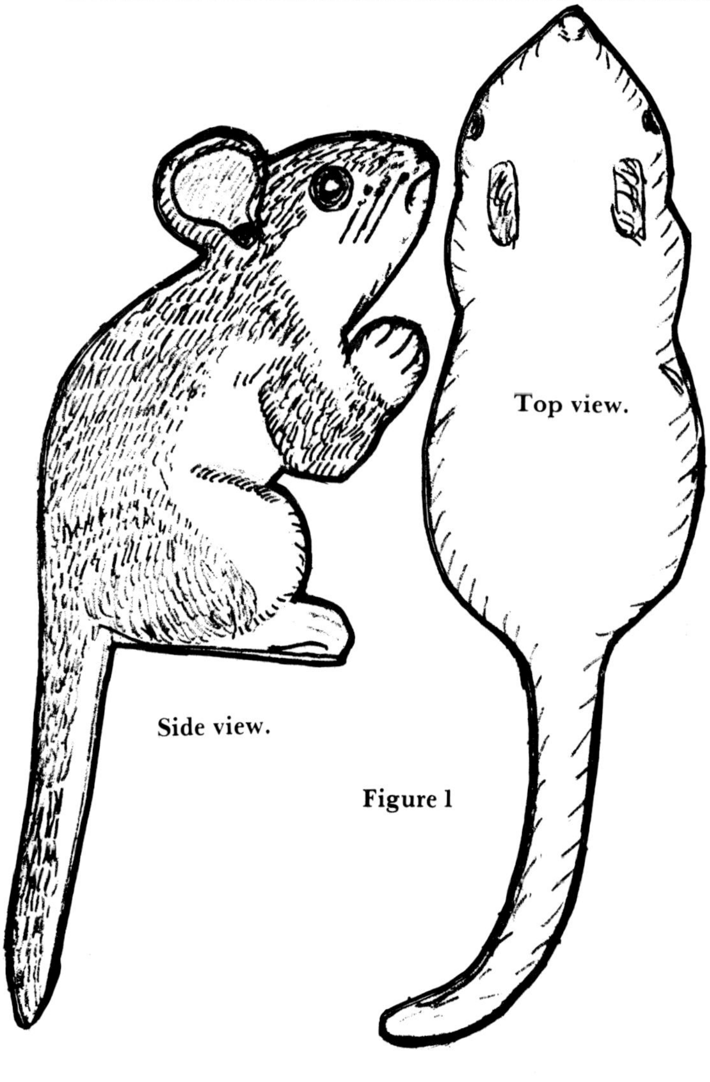

Figure 1

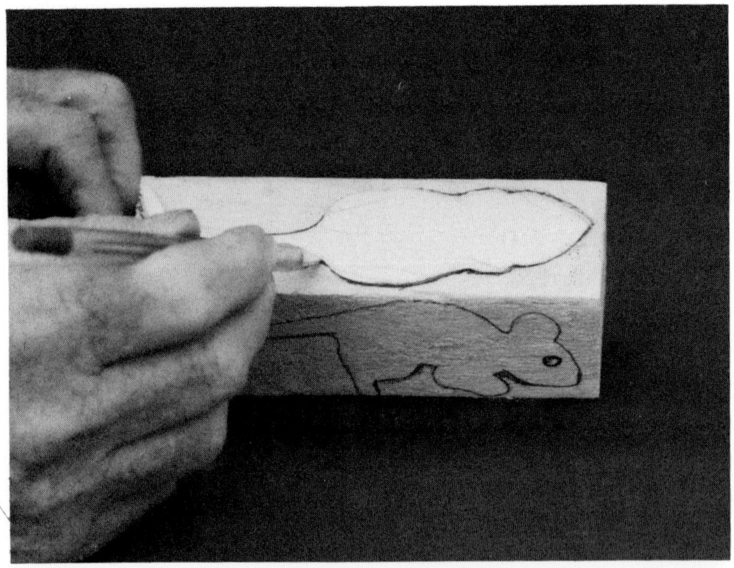

Figure 2

Trace top view on basswood block.

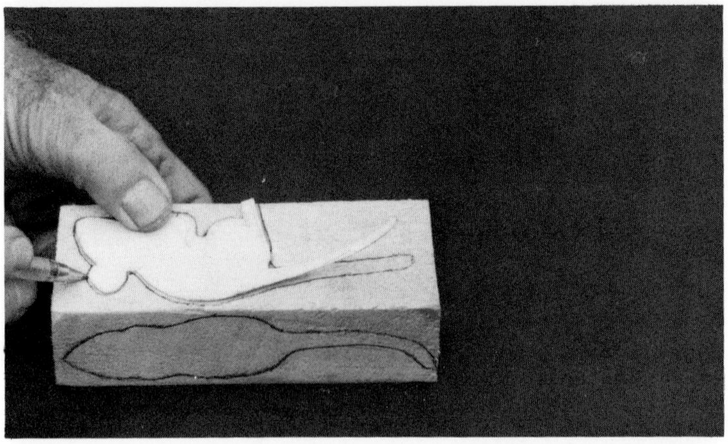

Figure 3

Trace side view on block as shown.

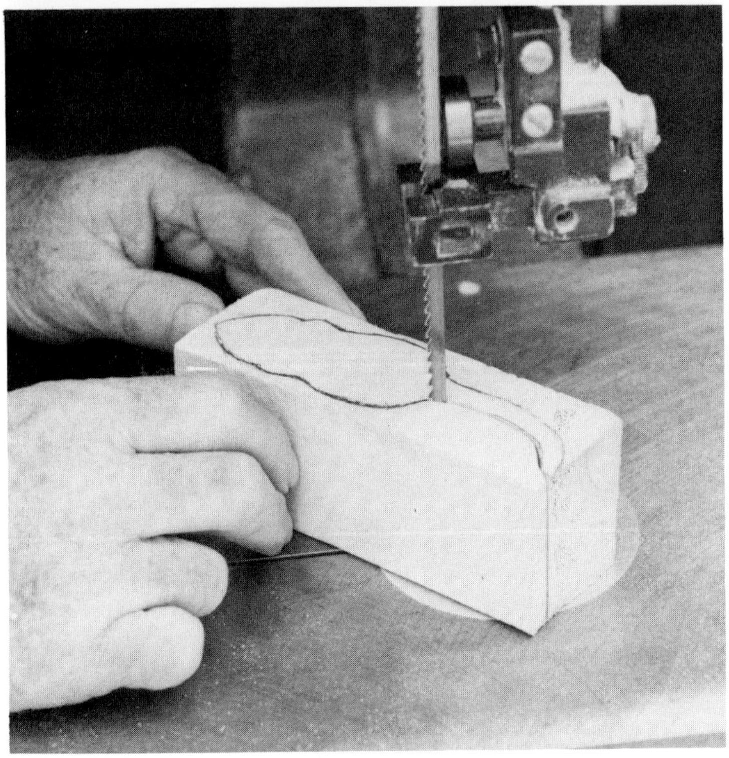

Figure 4

Cut out the top view of the carving. Start at the tail and leave the block intact by stopping at the nostril.

Figure 5

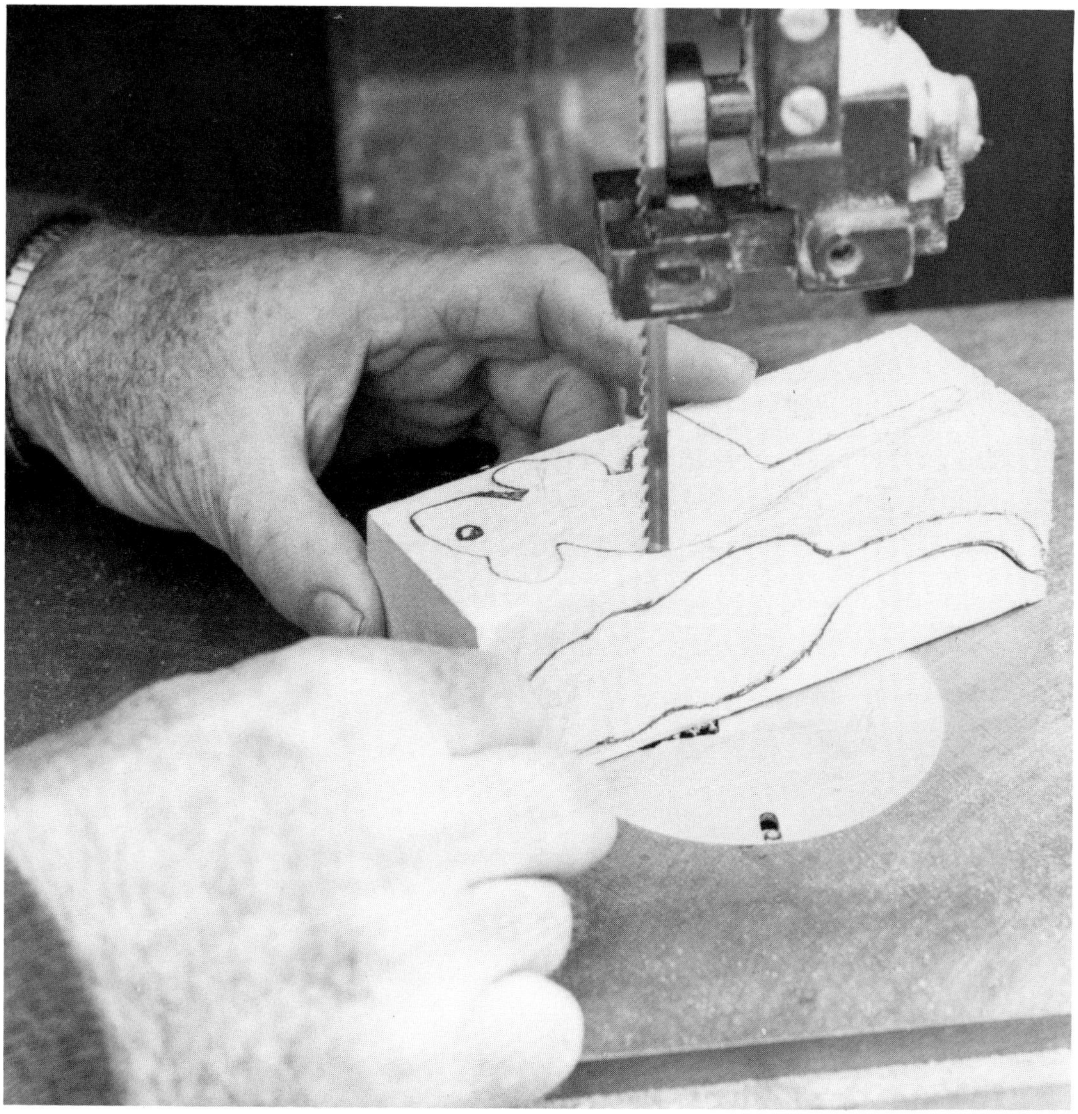

Cut out the side view completely as shown.

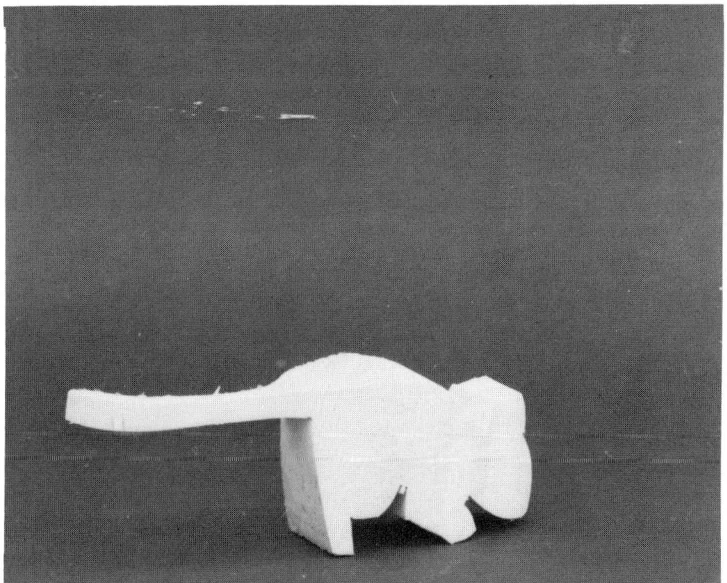

Figure 6

Side view of cut out.

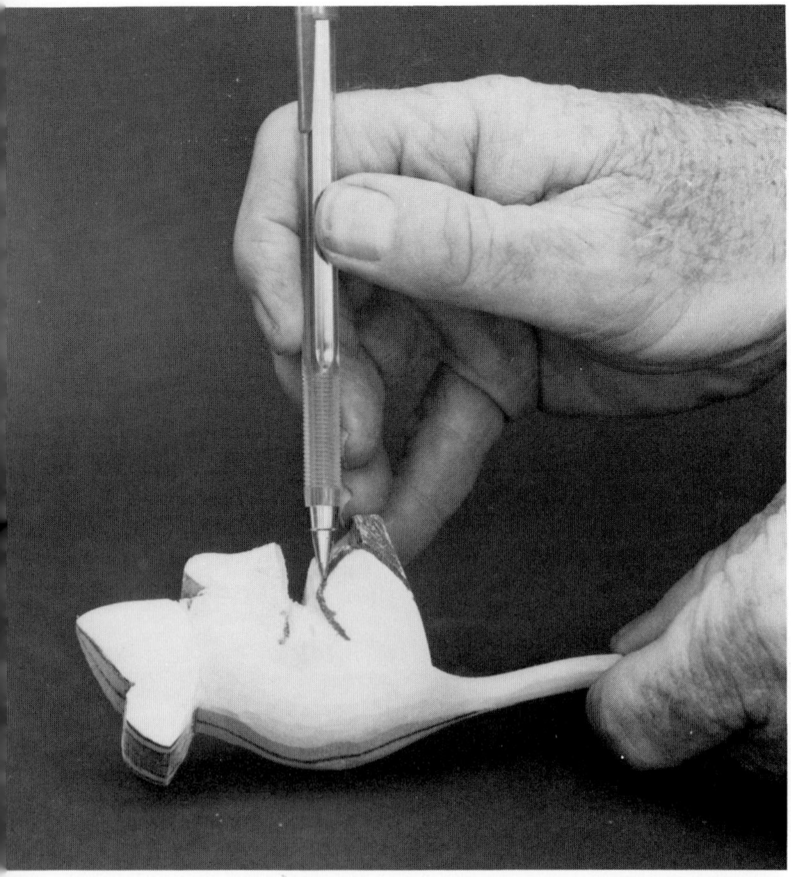

Figure 7

Using a carving knife, round out the back, head and tail. Lightly sand with drum sander on the moto-tool. Mark in the outline of the hips and upper legs, as shown.

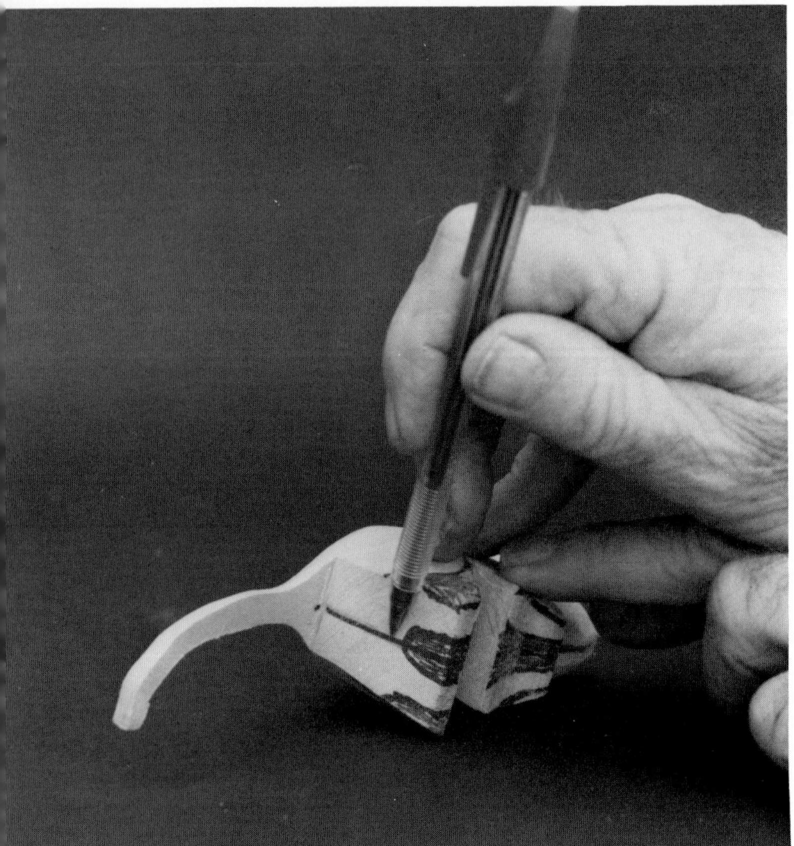

Figure 8

Block out the area to be removed between the rear legs and the upper legs as shown.

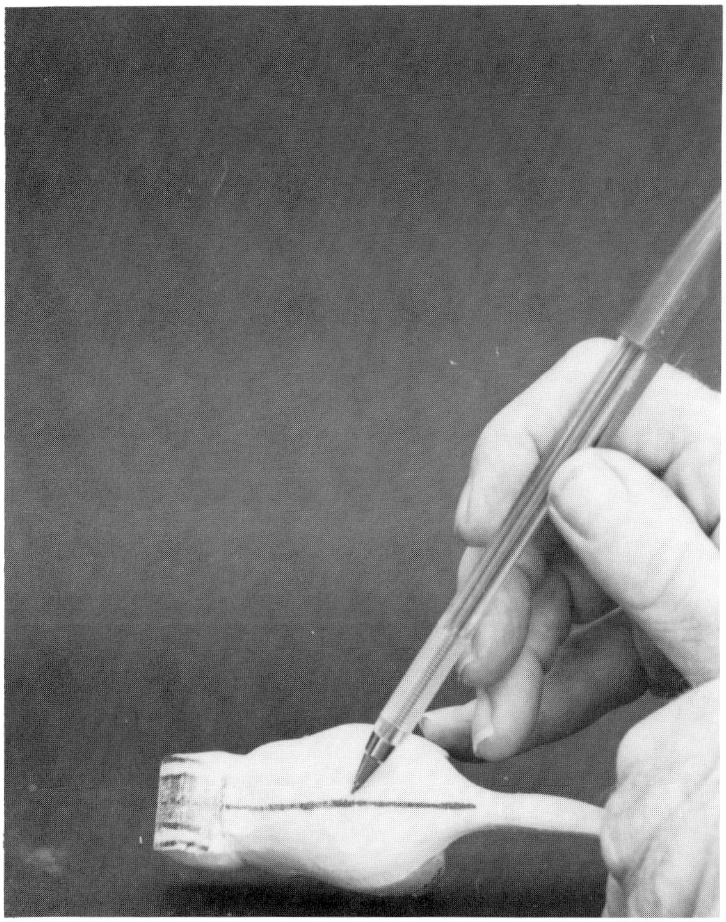

Figure 9

Block out the area to be removed between the ears as shown.

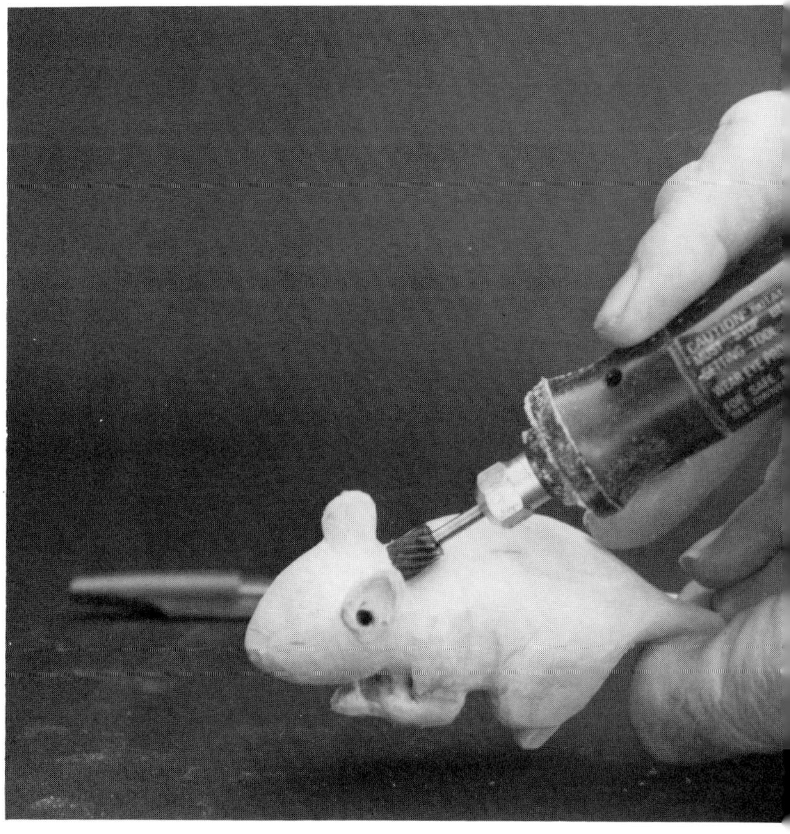

Figure 10

Using Dremel cutting heads carve out area between the ears and scoop out the cave in the ears leaving a slight rim as shown.

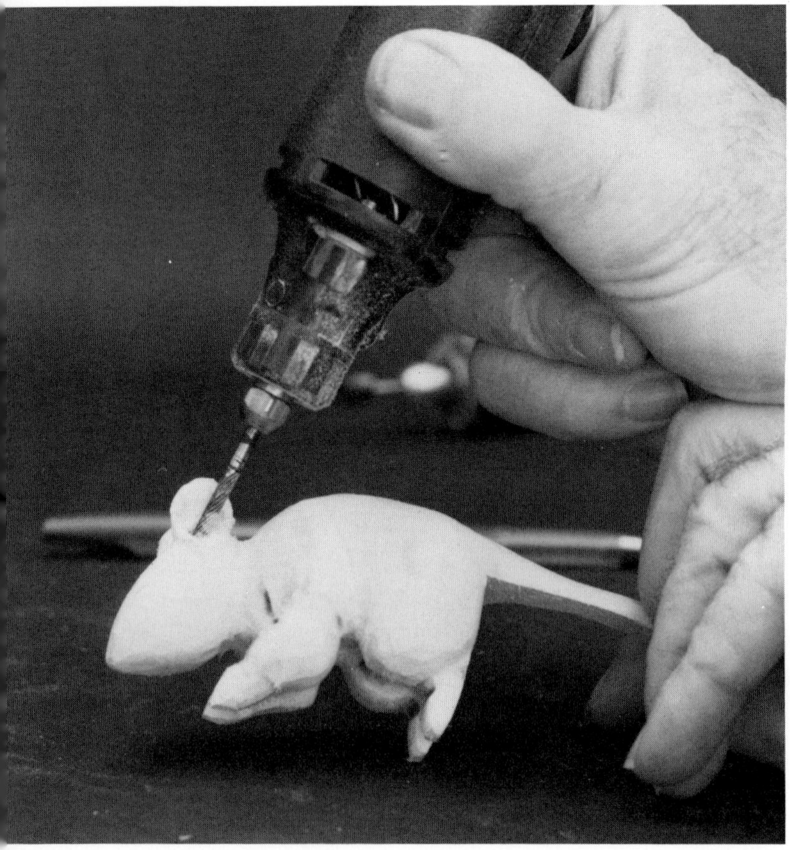

Figure 11

Using 1/8 inch drill, insert a hole in the base of each ear.

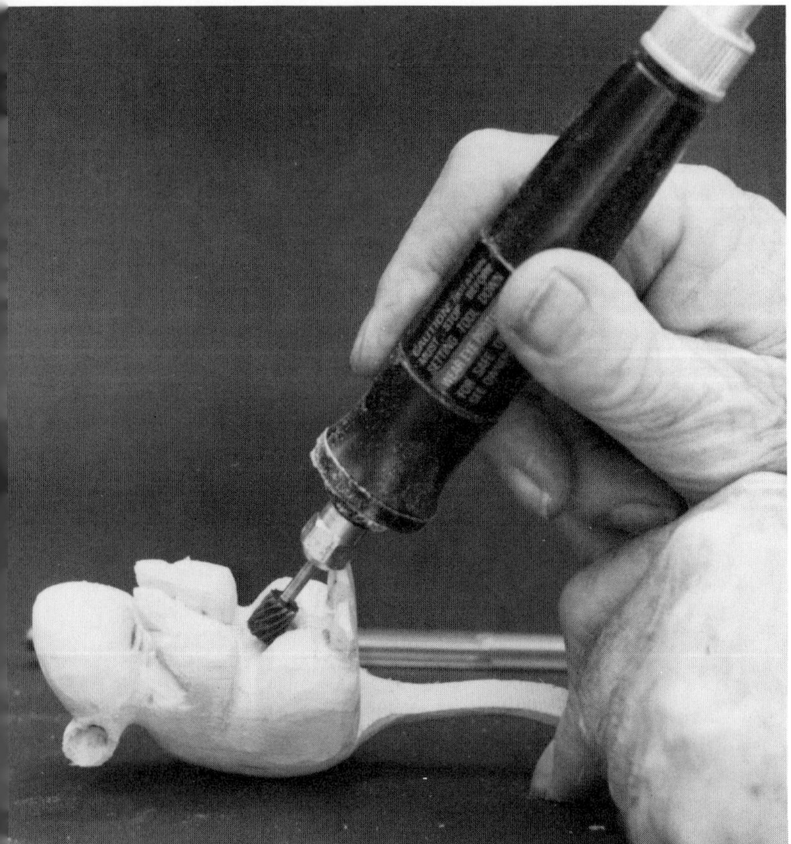

Figure 12

Carve the area between the legs as shown rounding out the hips on the rear legs and front legs.

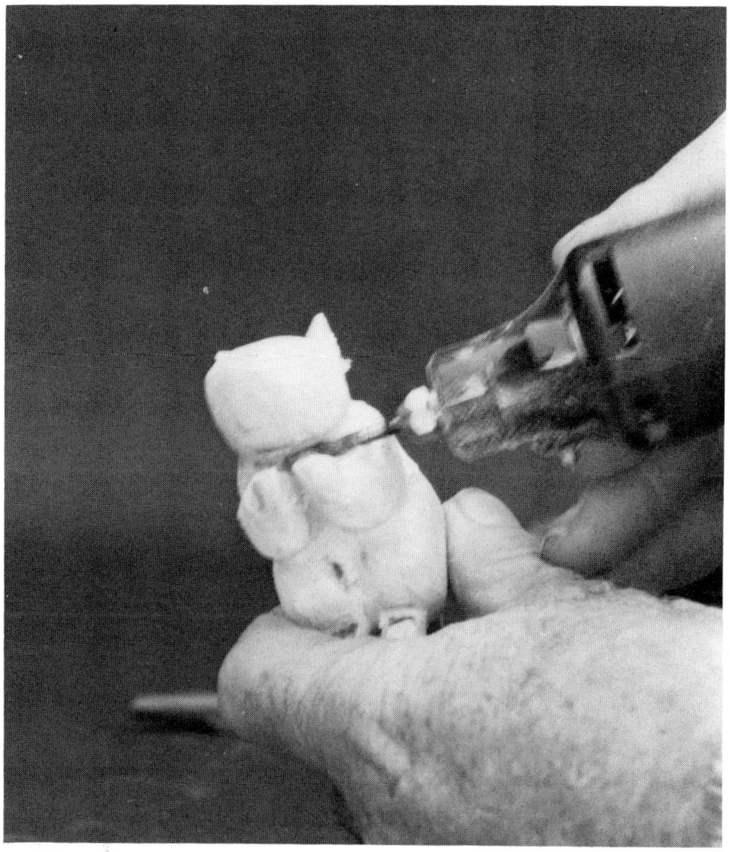

Figure 13

Carve the area under the head using cutting head No. 115 as shown. Hand sand the entire carving with fine sand paper.

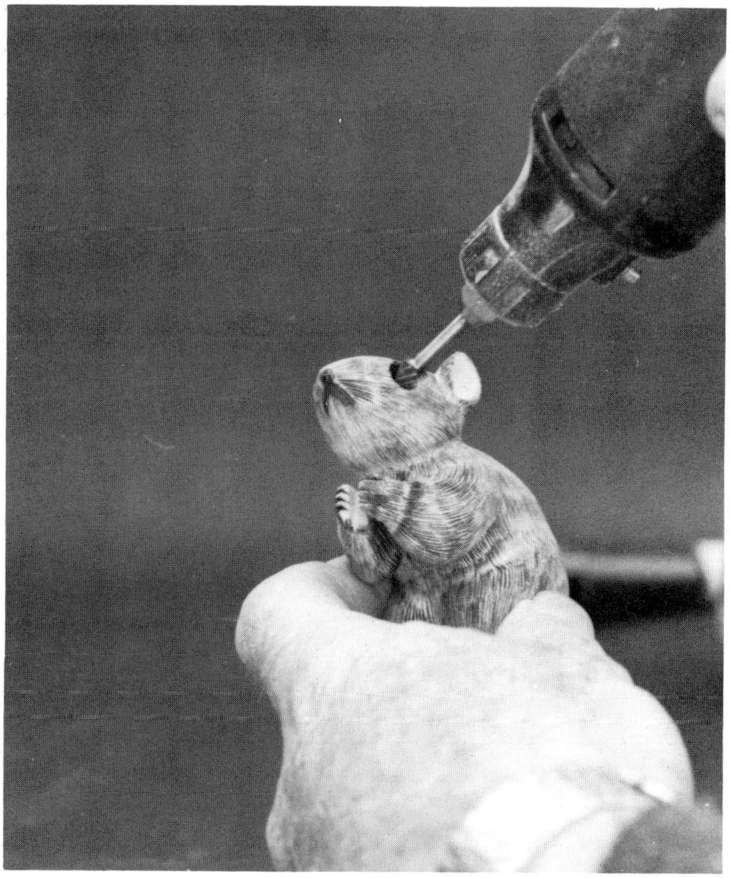

Figure 14

The carving textured with a burning pen. Note the "burned-in" shape of the mouth and toes. Use short strokes with the pen to indicate the furry appearance, keeping the strokes close together. Drill the eye socket with cutting head No. 125.

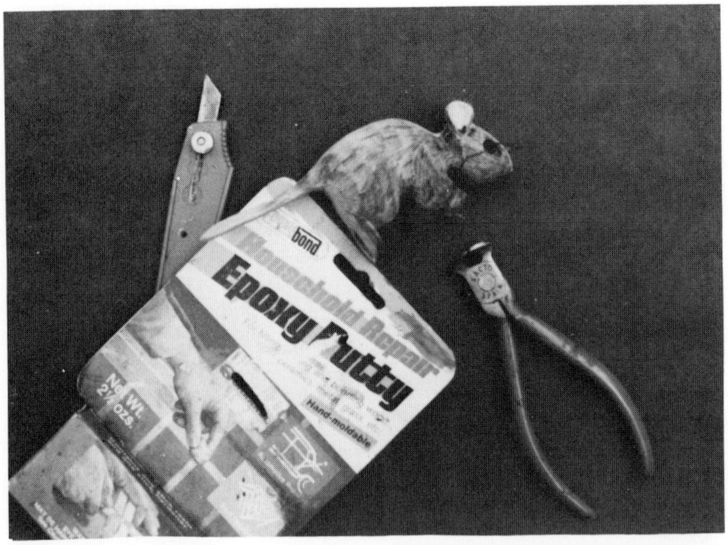

Figure 15

Paint the clear glass eyes (3 mm) with burnt umber. Shown here are the tools and epoxy putty used to install the eyes.

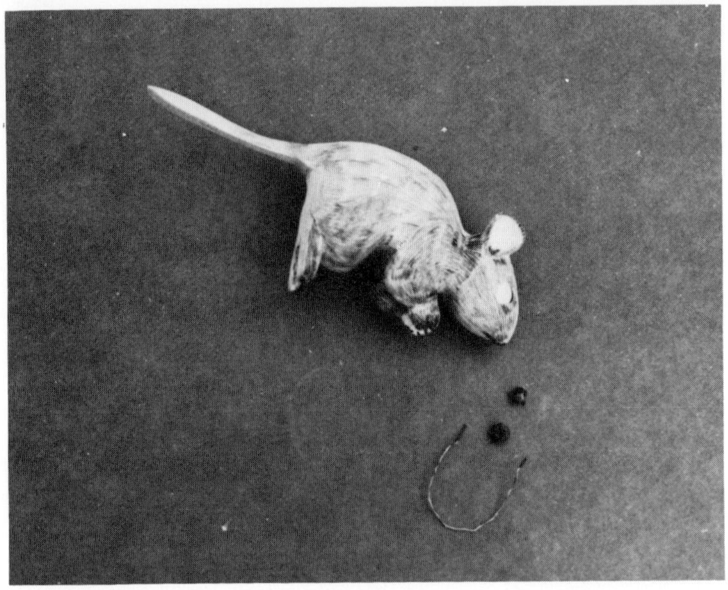

Figure 16

Fill the eye holes with putty and clip off the wire.

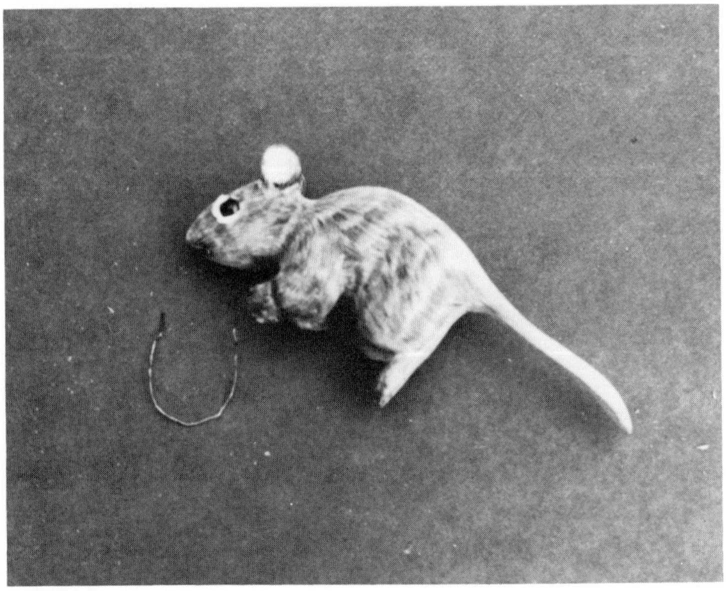

Figure 17

Smooth out putty and form a light lid.

Lightly mark four toes on each paw and burn the marks with the burning pen.

Paint the entire carving with titanium white and a slight touch of raw sienna. Dry with hair dryer.

Paint the upper part of the head through the back and down through the tail using raw sienna and a slight touch of burnt sienna.

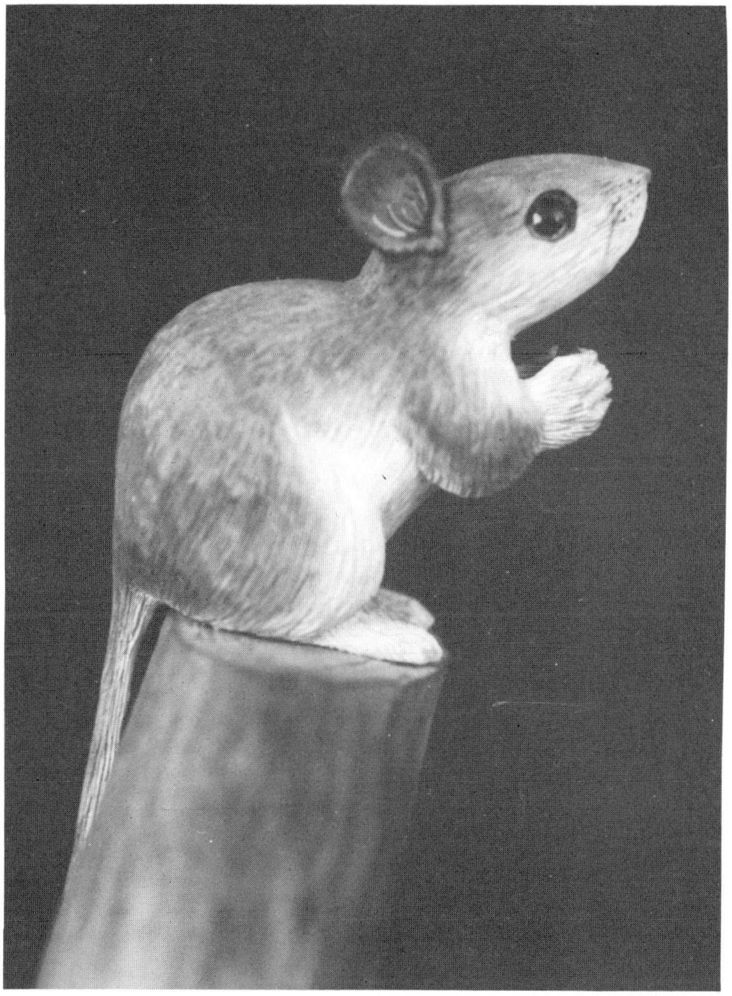

Figure 18

Use the same mix and paint the hips on the legs as shown in figure 18 and color figure 18.

Dry brush the transition areas between the white and raw sienna to eliminate the sharp line of demarkation.

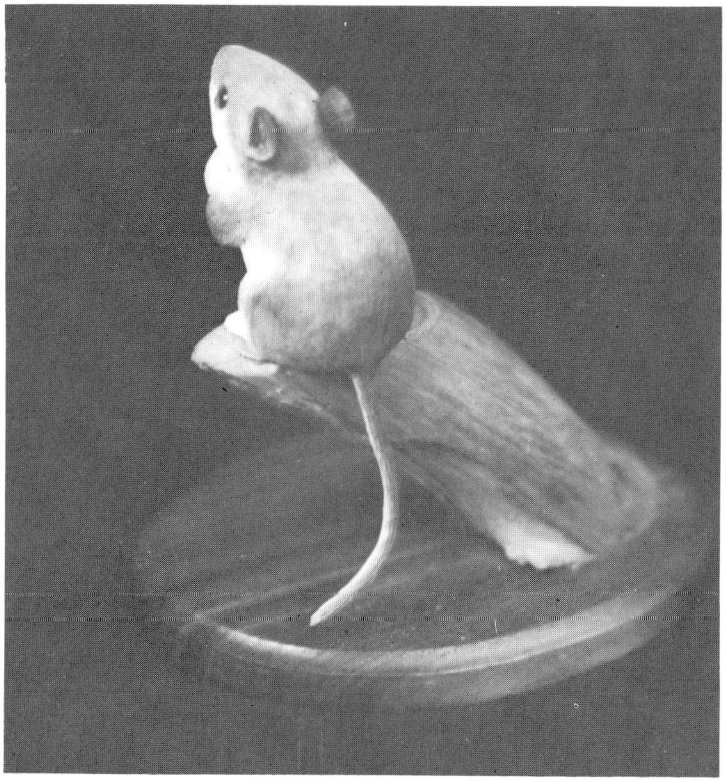

Figure 19

The back of the painted carving. A touch of burnt sienna is used to paint the caves of the ears. (See color figure 19).

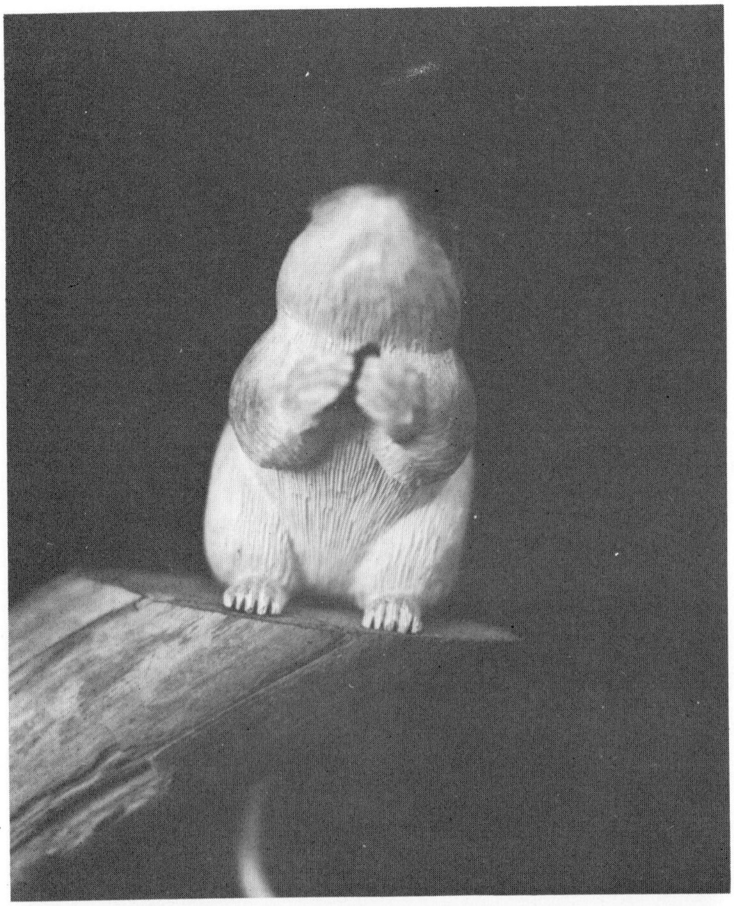

Figure 20

Front view of the wood mouse. (See color figure 20).

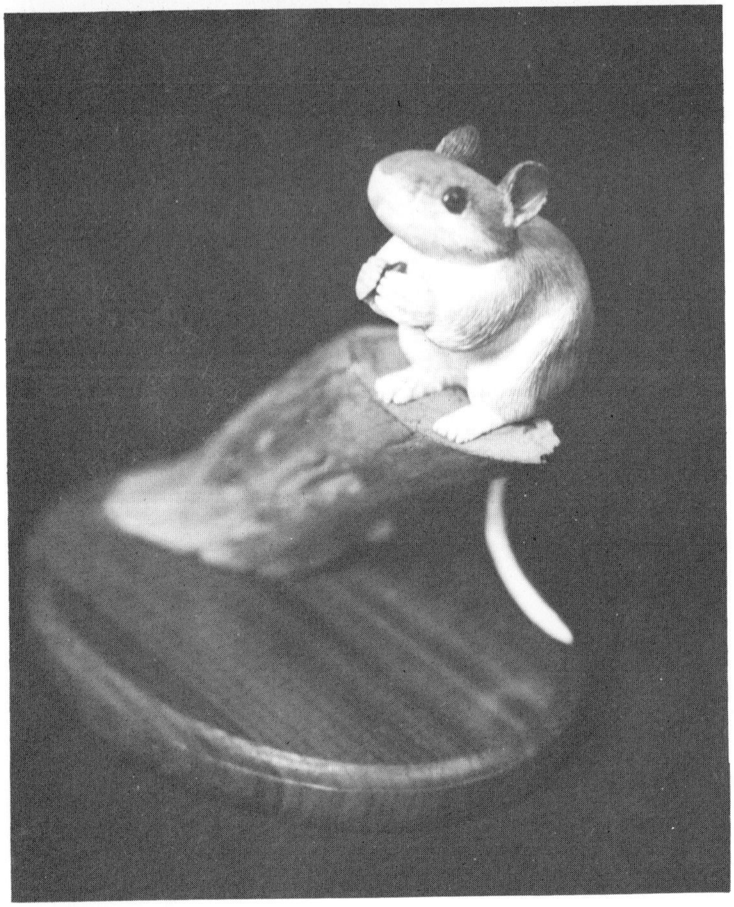

Figure 21

Insert whiskers about 3/4 inch long around the snout. Carve a sunflower seed and insert in upper paws. Mounted carving shown on short oak branch on maple base. (See color figure 21).

The Great Horned Owl, Relief Carving

Materials And Tools Needed

Basswood block 6" x 4" x ½"
9 mm clear glass eyes
Carving knives (X-acto Relief)
Epoxy Putty

Moto-tool
Cutting heads
Nos. 115, 116, 124, 125, & 194
Drum sander with fine sanding band

Sandpaper
Rubbing alcohol
Low gloss Tung Oil
Protective clear spray No. 370

This mature Great Horned owl *(Búbo virginiánus)* is 20 inches in length and has a wing spread of 55 inches. The ear tufts are larger and further apart and its belly is fine barred horizontally. This large headed, short-necked bird of prey is nocturnal and is best seen and heard at dusk. These owls hunt for rodents and other small mammals. Their calls are distinctive hoots, wails, or whistles.

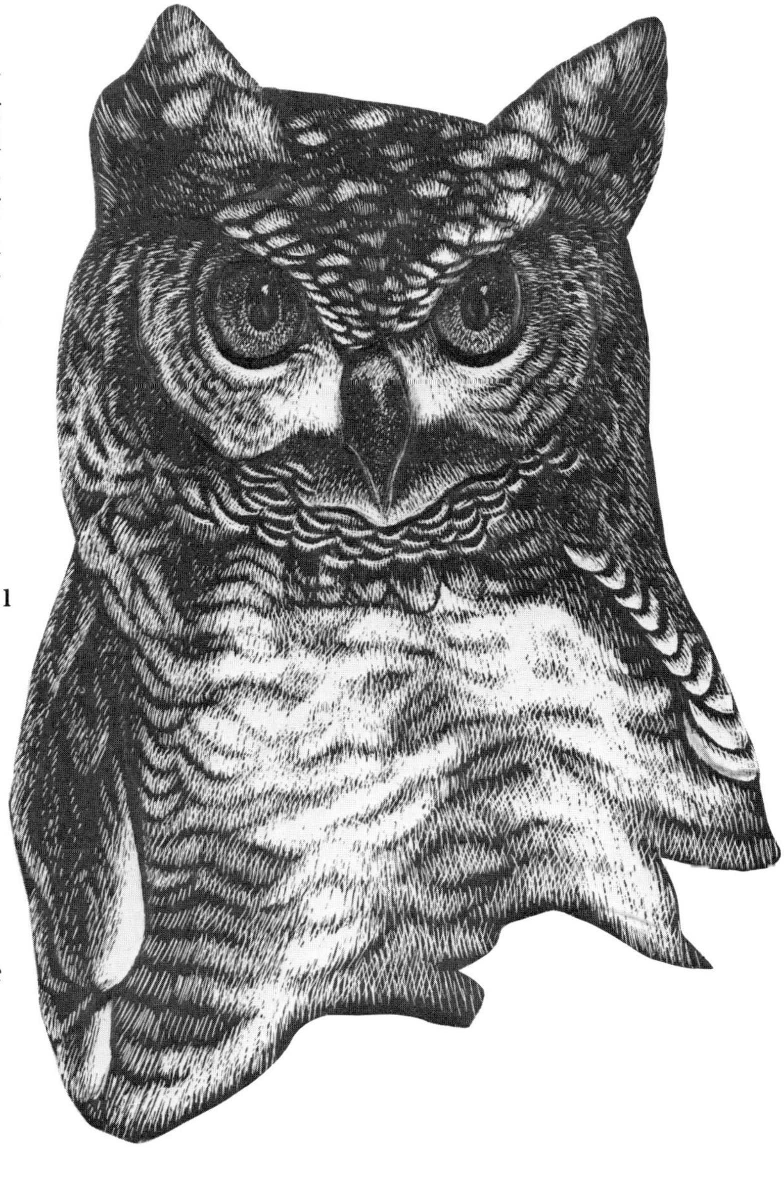

Figure 1

Using the pattern shown in figure 1, trace the pattern on the 6" x 4" x 1/2" basswood block.

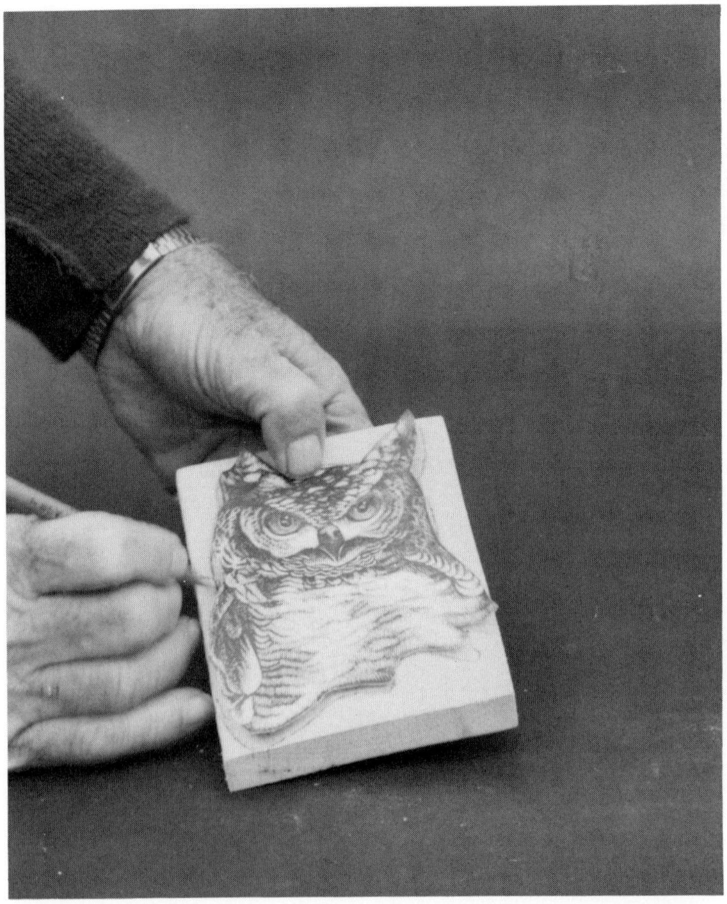

Figure 2

Trace the pattern.

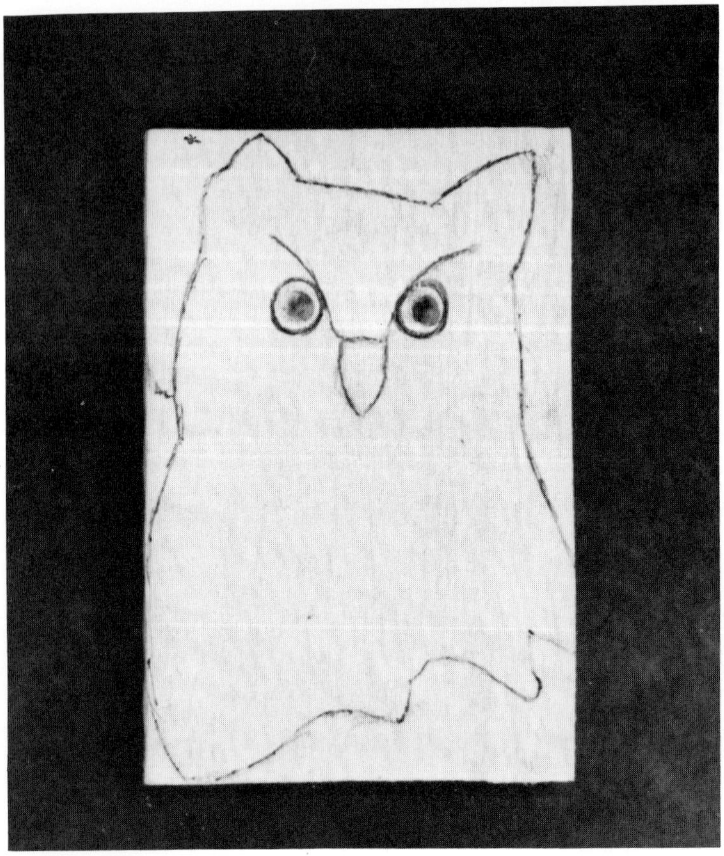

Figure 3

Using carbon paper trace the eyes, beak and lines as shown. Drill out the eye sockets using the moto-tool.

Figure 4

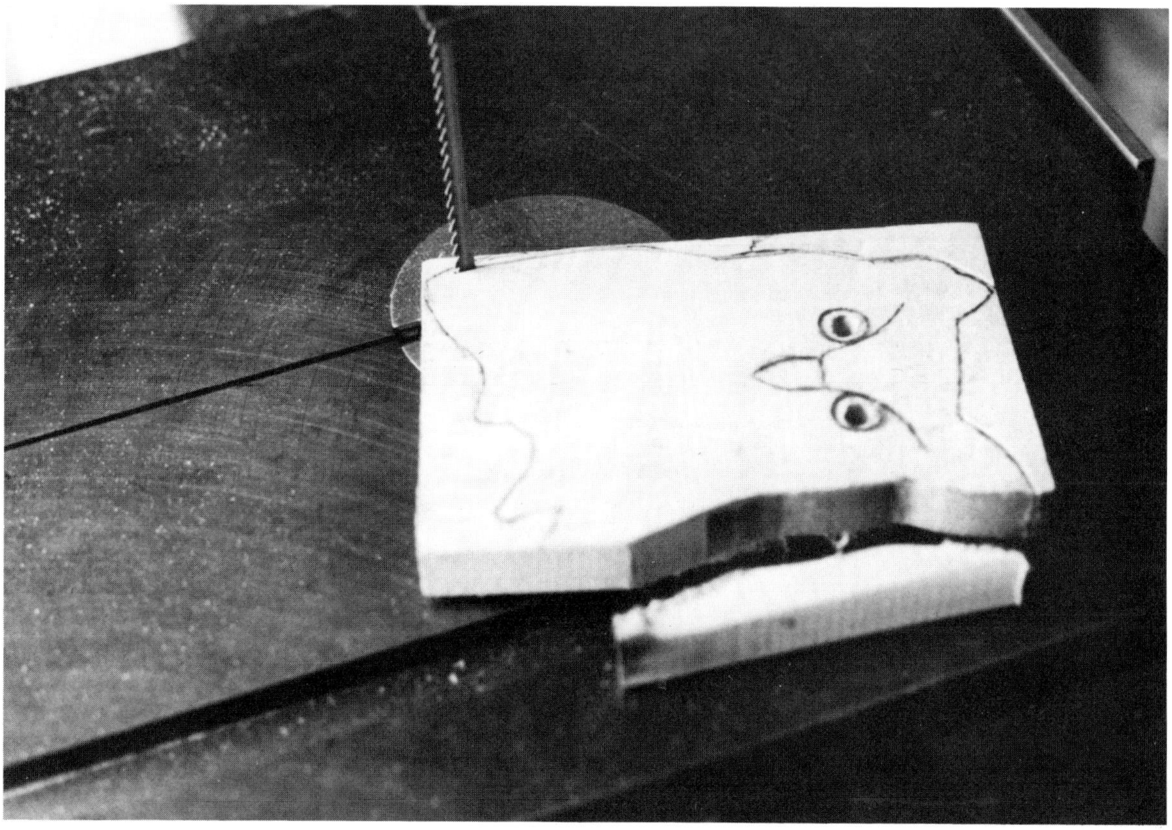

Cut out the owl as shown on bandsaw.

Figure 5

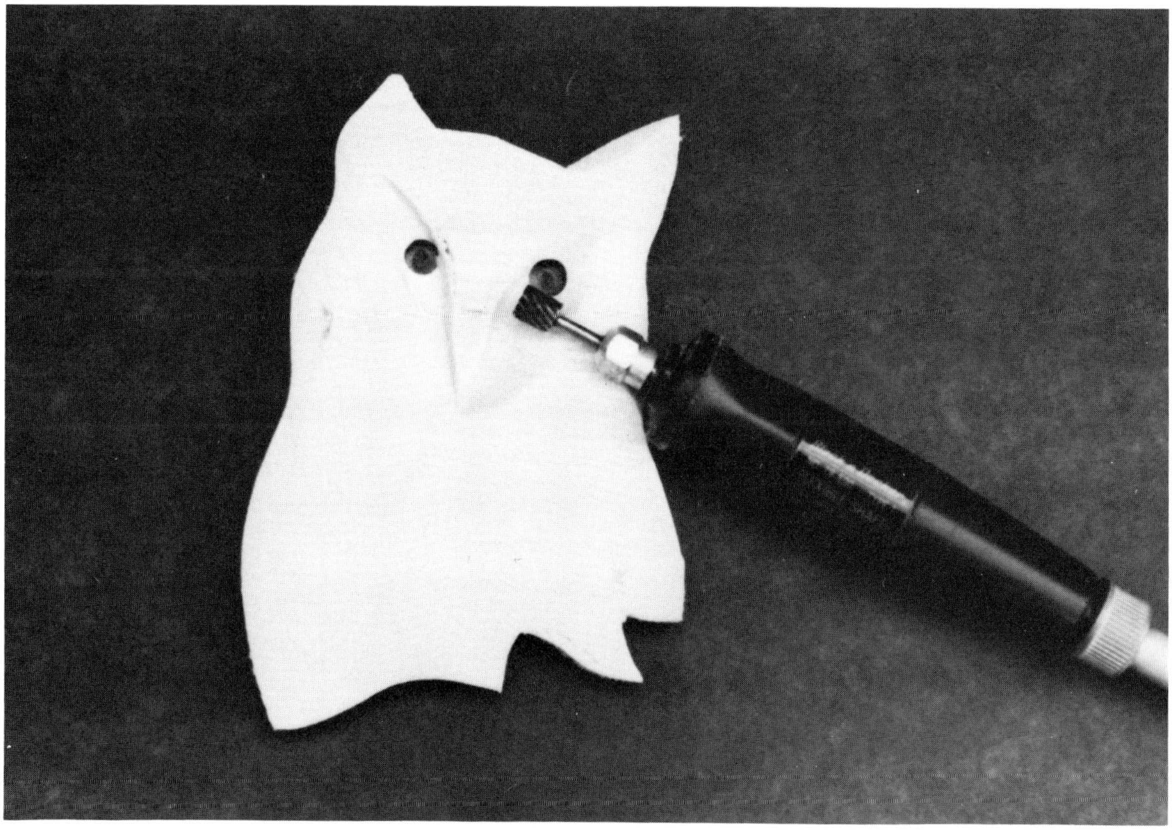

Using cutting bit No. 115, cut away the wood around the beak and the feather tuft above the eyes. Penetrate about 1/4 inch.

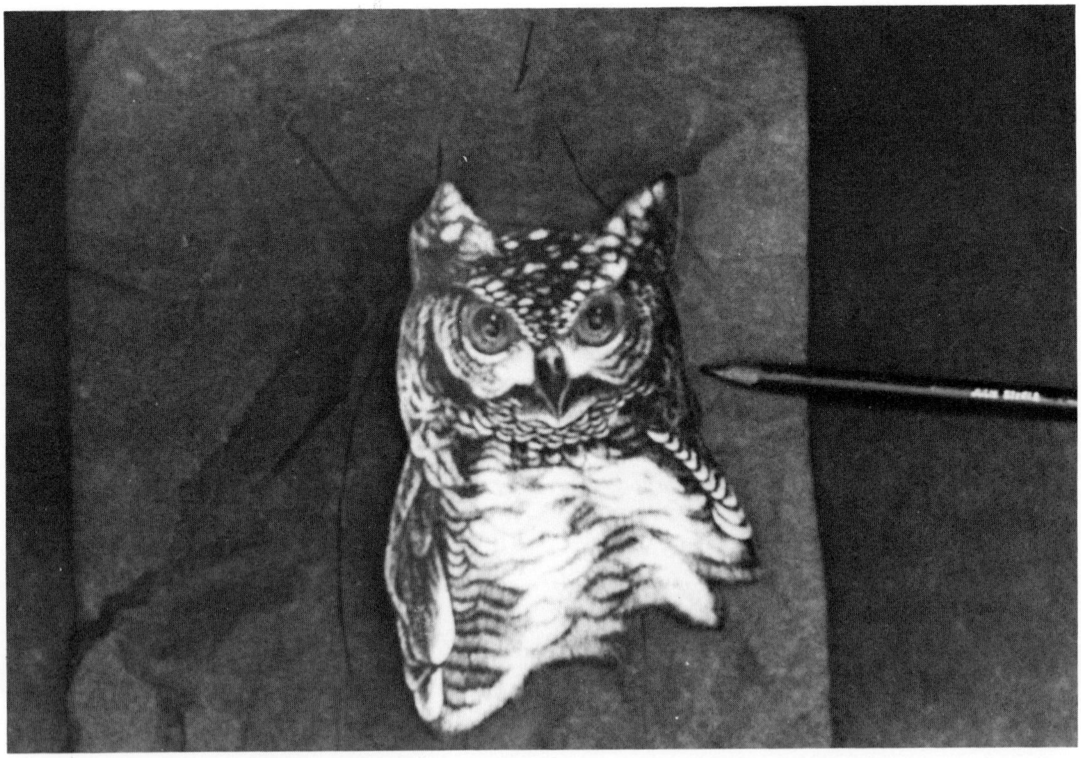

Figure 6

Trace the prominent lines on the head and wings using the pattern and carbon paper as shown.

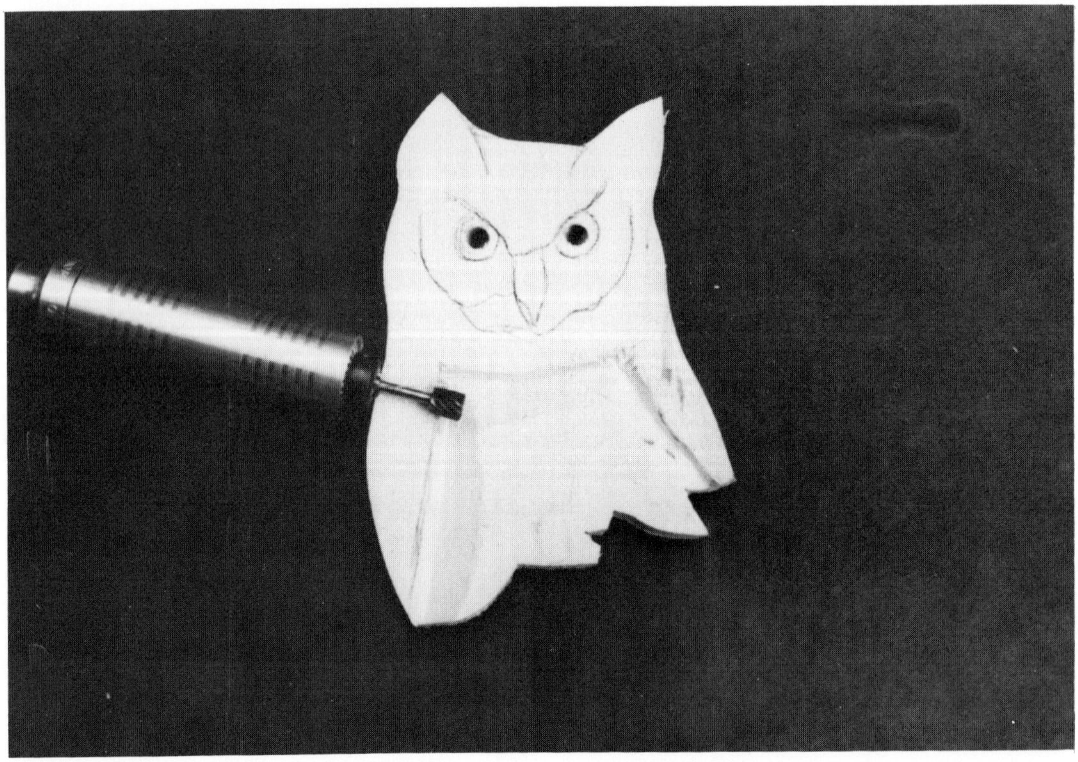

Figure 7

Using the moto-tool carve the side wings to a depth of 3/8 inch.

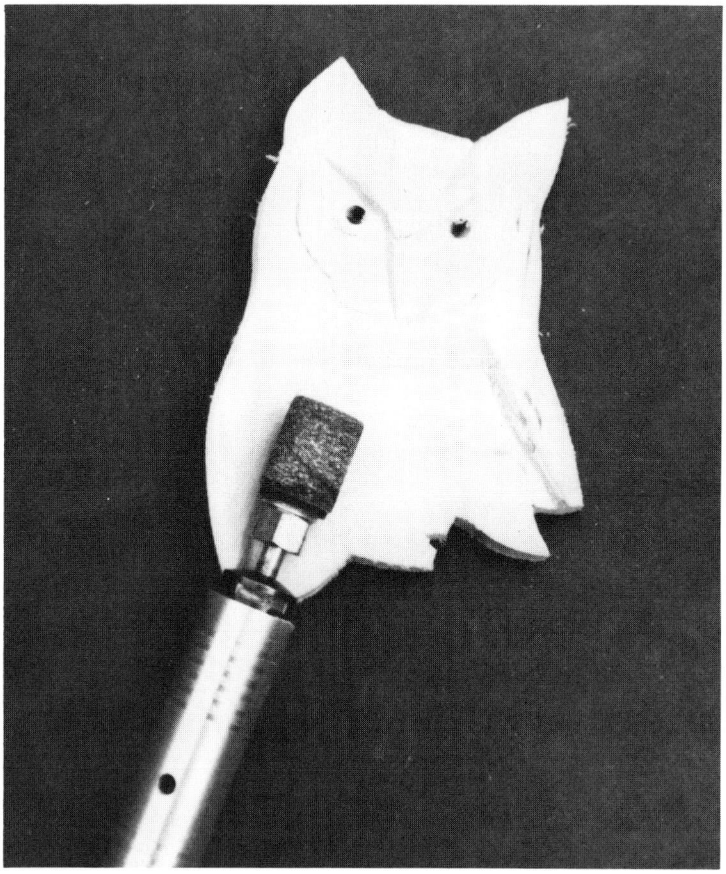

Figure 8

Using the drum sander round out the entire carving, ears, wings, head, and belly.

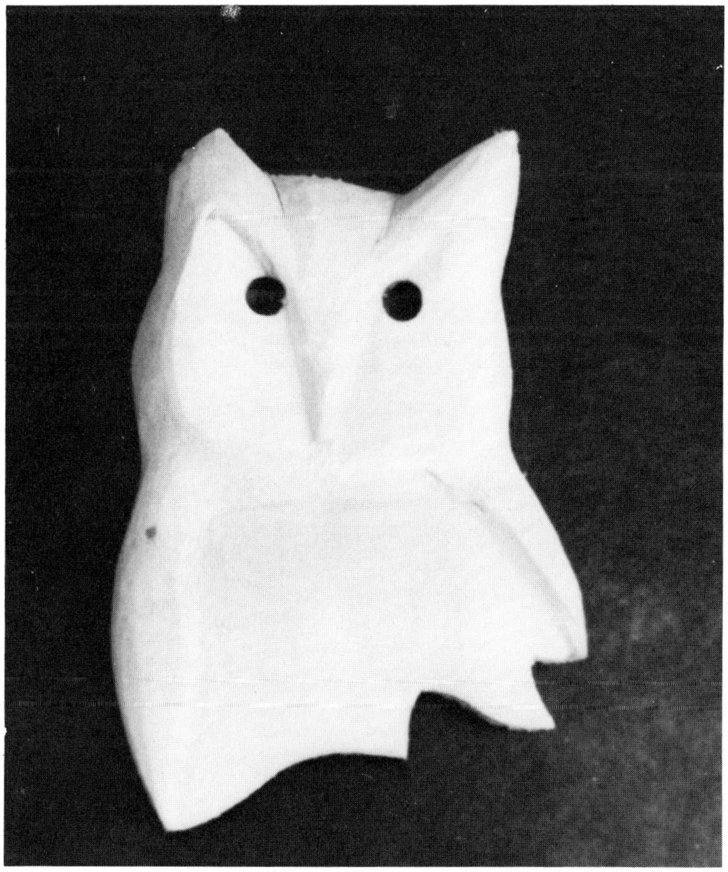

Figure 9

Use rubbing alcohol and fine hand sanding.

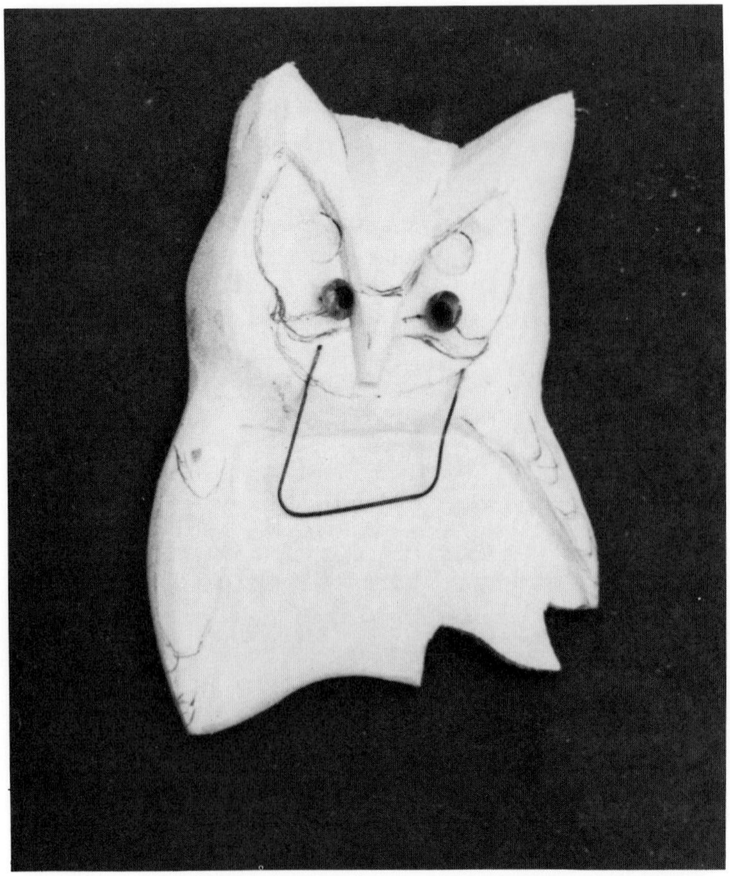

Figure 10

Paint the crystal glass eyes yellow. Drill eye sockets and check the holes for size.

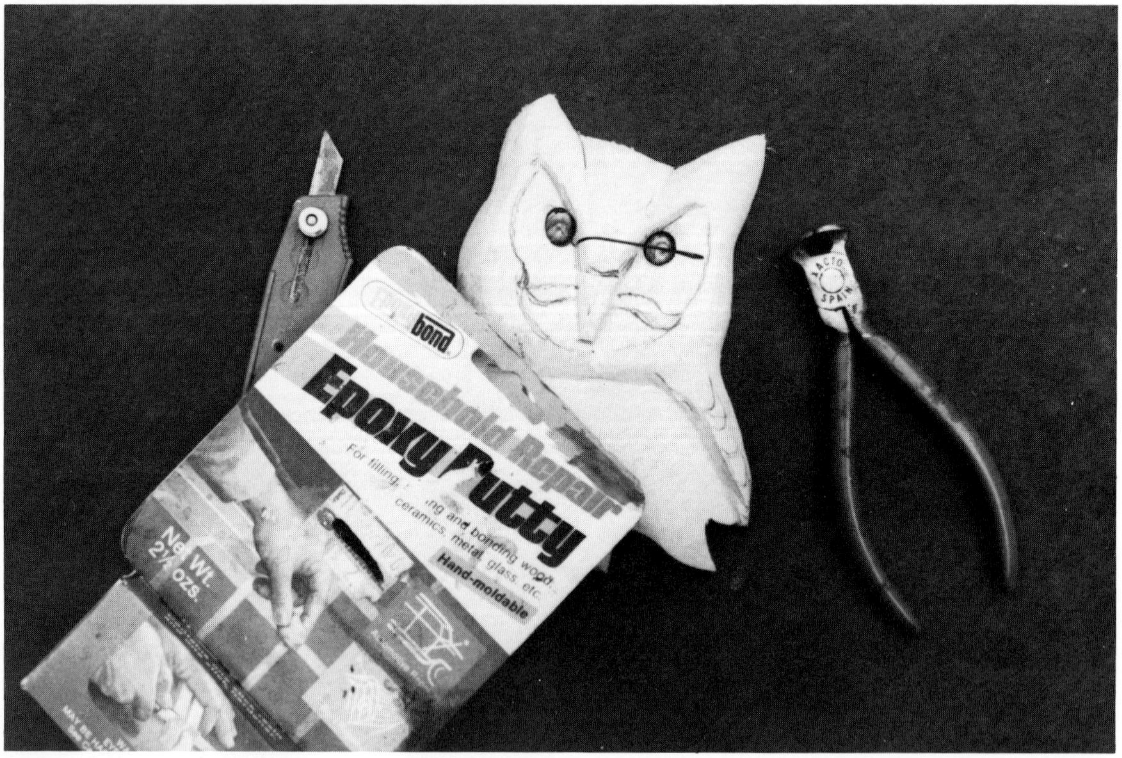

Figure 11

Fill sockets with putty and snip eyes leaving 1/4 inch of wire.

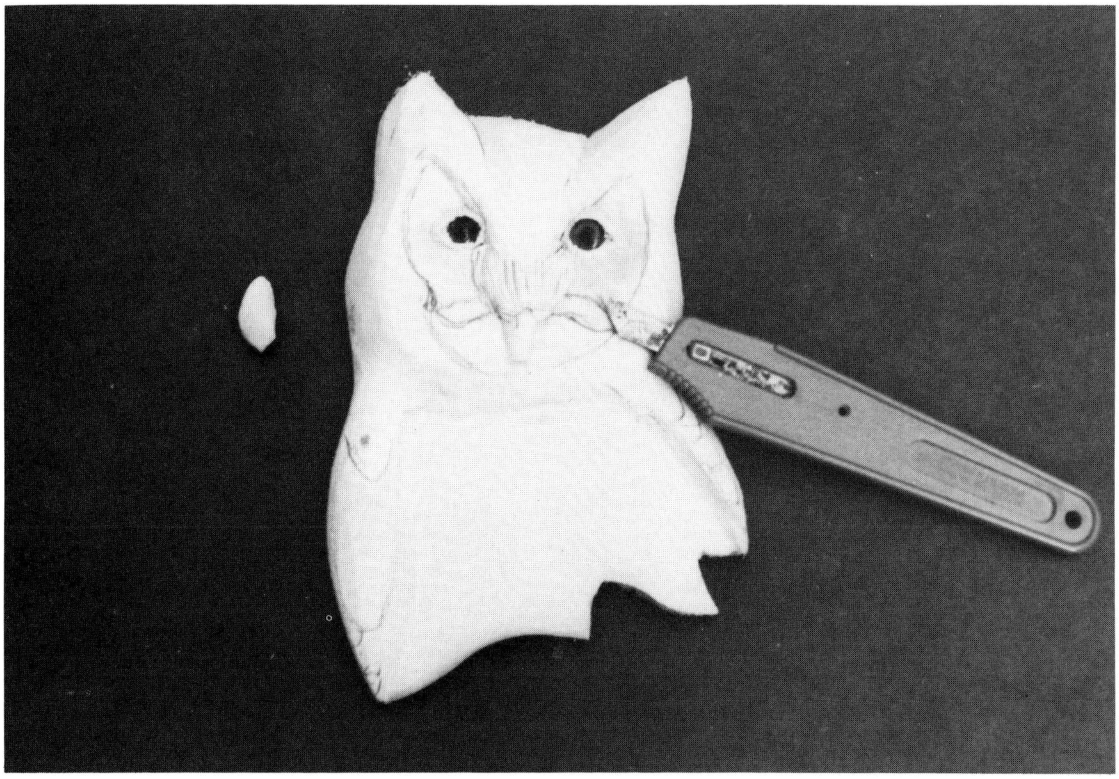

Figure 12

Insert eyes, shape eye lids, and apply putty around the area above the beak. This is to sculpture the feathery effect in this area.

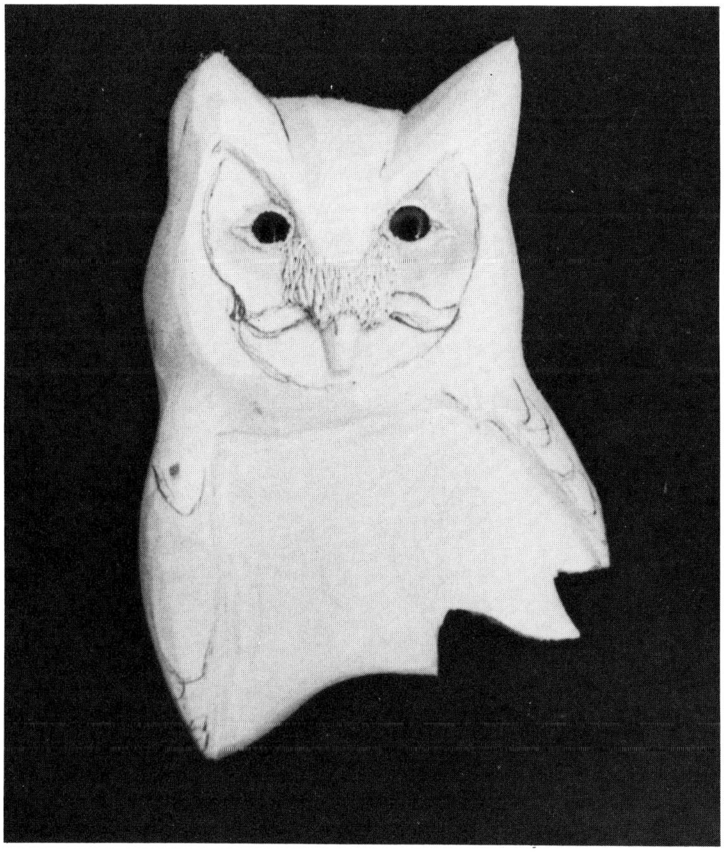

Figure 13

Using a knife point, stipple the feathery effect above the beak.

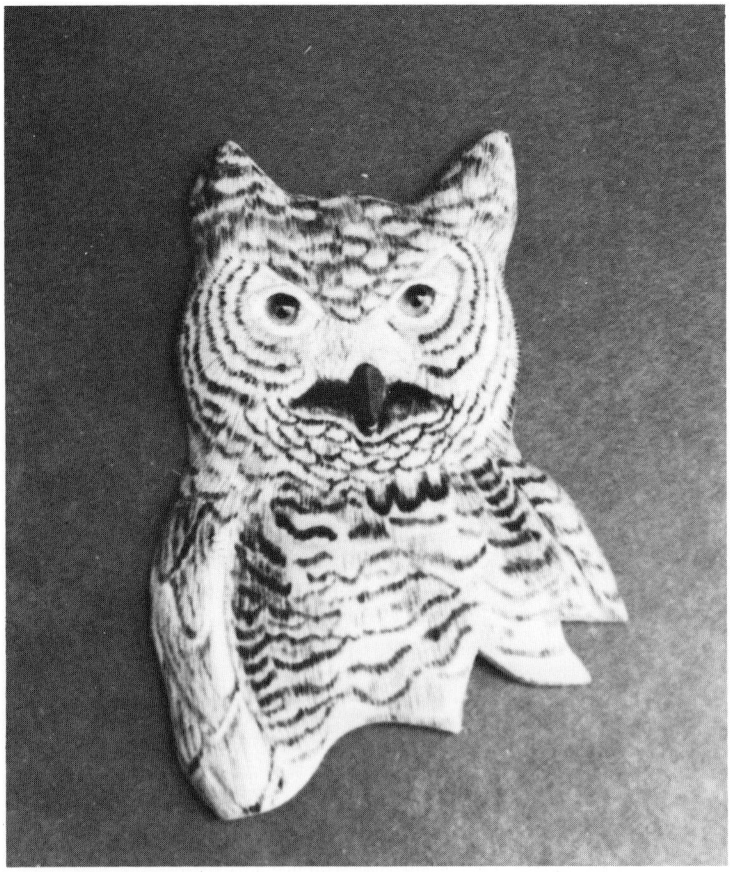

Figure 14

Pencil in the feather patterns on the carving and prepare it for texturing with a burning pen.

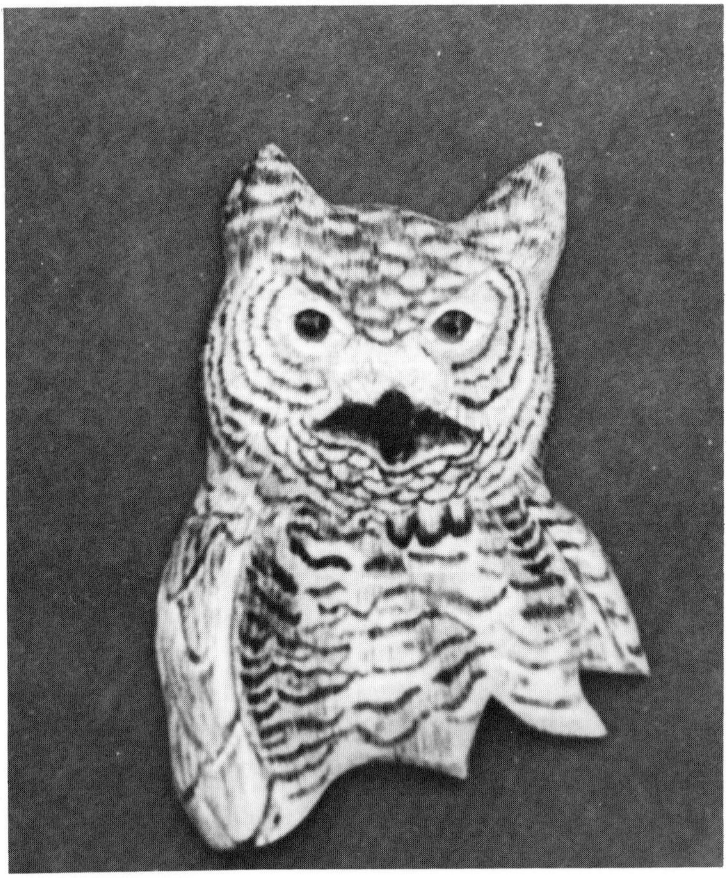

Figure 15

Burn the dark areas first using a high setting.

Set the pen on a very low setting and texture the light areas using compact strokes of the pen.

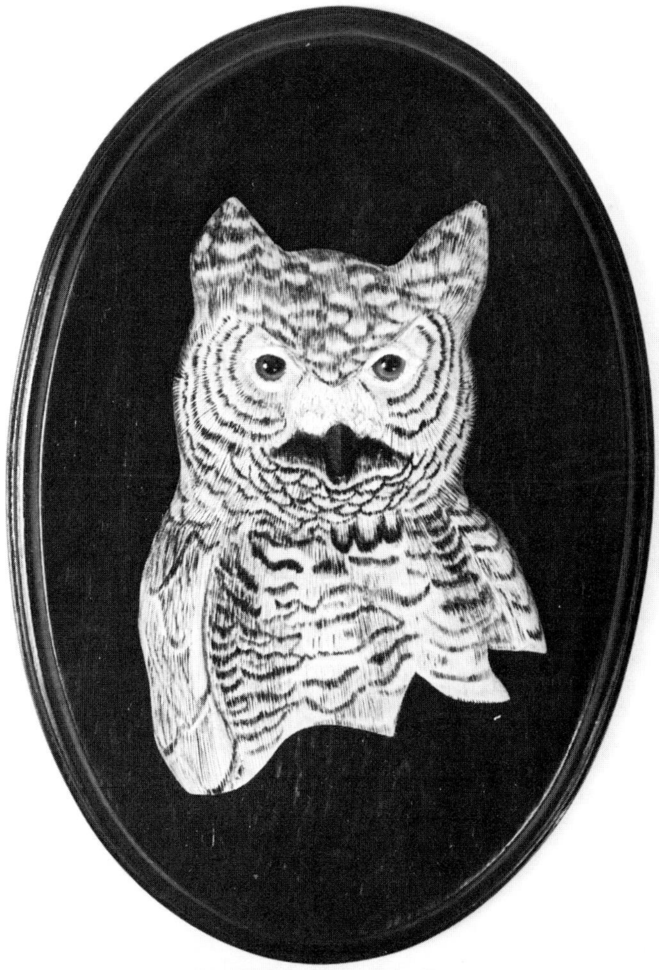

Figure 16

Bathe the carving in tung oil and rub with a soft cloth. Let it dry for a few hours and repeat the process. Spray with clear protective sealer and mount your relief carving on an appropriate base. (See color figure 16).

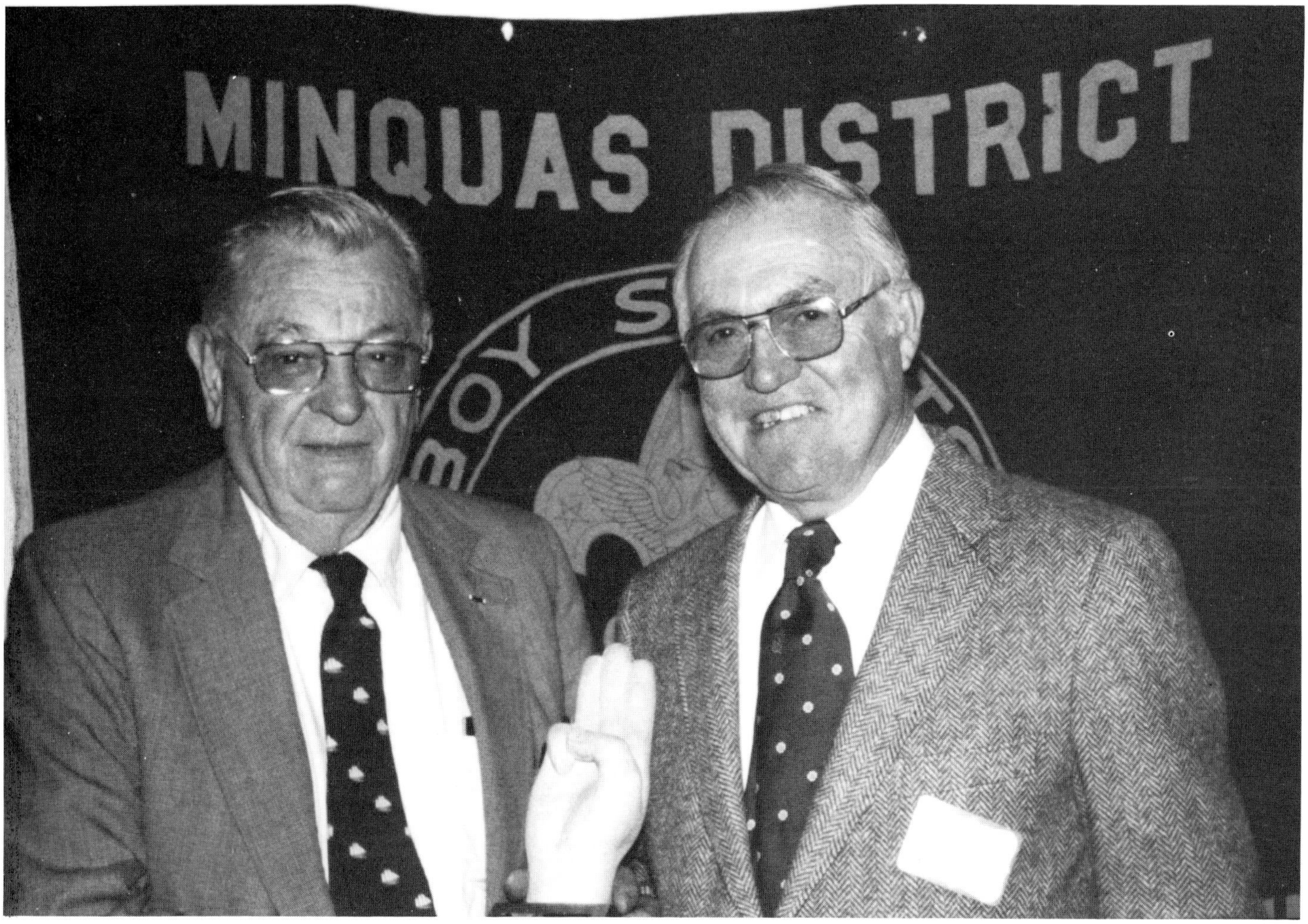

David Pergrin, right, presenting a carved Scouts salute to Senator Clarence Bell.

David E. Pergrin graduated from Pennsylvania State University in civil engineering. He commanded the legendary 291st Engineer Combat Battalion in World War II and was a Civil Engineer in the railroad industry for 35 years. He retired from his engineering career in 1979 when he served as an adviser to the Federal Rail Administration. He developed an Engineering Consulting Firm during the last 10 years of his active career.

Mr. Pergrin has been teaching wood carving for 15 years to the Boy Scouts of the Valley Forge Council in Pennsylvania. He developed the woodcarving program at the Scout Council's camp at Resica Falls where 500 boys each summer are involved in the program to receive their Wood Carving Merit Badge. The teaching of wood carving to the 7th and 8th graders at St. Johns Chrysostom Catholic school in Wallingford, Pennsylvania has developed many fine carvers in the past 7 years. He also enjoys teaching adults, both retired men and women as well as active persons in the working world. He feels that wood carving is an excellent therapy for all ages. *Woodcarving the Wonders of Nature* has been taught by Mr. Pergrin at the Nether Providence community classes, the Elder Craftsmen in Philadelphia, Pennsylvania, and at Tyler Arboretum in Lima, Pennsylvania.

In the course of his teaching career, Mr. Pergrin estimates he has instructed more than 10,000 carvers, many of whom have gone on to receive ribbons in carving competitions. He developed plans for the first annual Boy Scouts of America Carving Show in Wallingford, Pennsylvania in 1984. The success of that show will make it a yearly event.

Other carving and related books available from the publisher. Write for a free catalog.

Decoy Carving Techniques for the Intermediate Carver, by George Barber and Larry Reader.
Complete Waterfowl Studies, by Bruce Burk.
Volume I: *Dabbling and Whistling Ducks*
Volume II: *Diving Ducks*
Volume III: *Geese and Swans*
Waterfowl Carving: Blue Ribbon Techniques, by William Veasey and Cary Schuler Hull.
Waterfowl Painting: Blue Ribbon Techniques, by William Veasey.
Bills and Feet: An Artisan's Handbook, by William Veasey and Sina Kurman.
Blue Ribbon Pattern Series, by William Veasey.
I. *Full Size Decorative Decoy Patterns*
II. *Miniature Decoy Patterns*
III. *Head Patterns*
IV. *Song Bird Patterns*
V. *Shore Bird Patterns*
VI. *Miniature Decorative Patterns*
VII. *Hunting Birds*
VIII. *Birds of Prey*
Blue Ribbon Burning Techniques, by William Veasey.
Waterfowl Illustrated, by Tricia Veasey.
Championship Carving, by Tricia Veasey and Tom Johnson.

Other books in the Carvers' Handbook Series:

Volume I: *Woodcarving the Wonders of Nature.* (Chickadee, Chipmunk, Turtle, Nativity Relief)
Volume III: *Woodcarving the Action of the Plains*
(Indian neckerchief slide, Deer relief, Horse stallion, Cardinal)